PRAISE FOR
Positive Time-Out

"*Positive Time-Out* gives a fresh new perspective on time-out. Jane Nelsen gives parents and teachers the encouragement and tools they need to help children handle their own behavior. Parents who practice these principles are pleasantly surprised at their effectiveness and enjoy less conflict and more cooperation in the home."

—**Sheryl Hausinger, M.D., Texas Children's Pediatric Associates and mother of three**

"In *Positive Time-Out*, Jane Nelsen reminds us that children 'do better' when they feel better. Don't we all? The key is using kindness and firmness at the *same time*. The book offers more than 50 ways that parents can set limits while still encouraging their kids. It should be in every doctor's waiting room."

—**Jody McVittie, M.D., family physician**

"Teaching children and adults the value of positive time-out is a gift that can serve them throughout their lives. Getting rid of rewards and punishment is essential for time-out to be helpful to children. This book is a must have for both teachers and parents."

—**Kay Rogers, retired elementary teacher and Positive Discipline associate**

"As I read *Positive Time-Out* I kept saying 'Yes!' Finally, it's 'time-in' for time-out as one of the many useful positive discipline tools introduced here. Adults will welcome this tool for their own use, as well as for the children! Children today need adults who are encouraging and respectful teachers and this book is written for them. Move over punishment and reward! It's high time for *Positive Time-Out*."

—**Mary L. Hughes, Family Life Field Specialist, Iowa State University Extension**

ALSO IN THE
POSITIVE DISCIPLINE SERIES

Jane Nelsen, Ed.D.

Positive
Time-Out

And Over 50 Ways to
Avoid Power Struggles in
the Home and the Classroom

 THREE RIVERS PRESS • NEW YORK

Published by Three Rivers Press, New York, New York.
Member of the Crown Publishing Group, a division of Random House, Inc.
www.randomhouse.com

THREE RIVERS PRESS and the Tugboat design are registered trademarks of Random House, Inc.

Originally published by Prima Publishing, Roseville, California, in 1999.

Illustrations by Paula Gray

Printed in the United States of America

Library of Congress Cataloging-in-Publication Data
Nelsen, Jane.
    Positive time-out : and over 50 ways to avoid power struggles in the home and the classroom / Jane Nelsen.
        p.   cm.
    Includes bibliographical references and index.
    1. Discipline of children. 2. Timeout method. 3. Child rearing.
4. School discipline. 5. Classroom management. I. Title.
HQ770.4.N439   1999
649'.64—dc21   99-41663
                                                                            CIP

ISBN 0-7615-2175-5

10 9 8 7 6 5
First Edition

To my daughter, Lisa McCaslin,
who loves her two children enough to be a learner
and who shares her delight when "it works."

CONTENTS

ACKNOWLEDGMENTS

FOR ELEVEN YEARS, Susan Madden (who thinks my faults are endearing) has been my valuable assistant and friend. She encourages me, protects me, and is a fabulous editor. Thanks, Susan.

I feel privileged to have Jamie Miller as my Prima editor. Jamie has the ability to wear different hats to advise me in whatever ways I need encouragement. And, thanks, Jamie, for taking the extra time to brainstorm with me in areas that need special creativity.

Tara Mead is an excellent copy editor and project manager who knows what needs to be changed, moved around, or just plain deleted to create a better book. Thanks, Tara.

It is with special gratitude that I acknowledge Lynn Lott, my co-author on several books and my friend. Lynn pushed me to go beyond my comfort level to engage in role-plays and activities that helped me "get into the child's world" to truly understand the negative, long-range effects of punitive methods—and the positive long-range effects of kind and firm (positive-discipline) methods. Thanks, Lynn, you have made the world a better place.

I love writing with co-authors, and Cheryl Erwin is one of the best. Her way with words brings the text to life and can move readers to laughter or tears. Cheryl made a tremendous contribution to this book in its self-published form, *Time-Out: Abuses and Effective Uses.* Cheryl, you are an incredible gift in my life.

I am especially indebted to the parents and teachers who attend my workshops and lectures. They truly care about children and want to encourage and empower them. They ask the questions and share the stories that keep us all learning and growing together in our desires and skills to work respectfully with children.

And then there is my husband Barry. Thank you isn't enough to express my gratitude for the love and support he gives—unconditionally. But, thank you will have to suffice for this setting.

Now, I want to take time-out to go hug my seventeen grandchildren.

ALTHOUGH TIME-OUT is one of the most popular disciplinary methods used in homes and schools, it is usually a humiliating and discouraging experience for children. This book explains how time-out can be a positive experience that empowers children to learn self-control and self-discipline while enhancing their self-confidence, courage, and self-reliance.

An Important Life Skill

KNOWING WHEN TO take time to calm down and cool off to gain access to inner wisdom and common sense is an important life skill. Instead of using time-out as punishment, adults can use it to teach children this important life skill.

Abuses and Effective Uses

WHEN I LEARNED that a school using isolation booths quoted *Positive Discipline* (Nelsen, 1996) as advocating time-out, I knew it was time for clarification. Although I do advocate time-out, I do so only when it is implemented in positive, encouraging, empowering ways, never as punishment.

This book aims to clarify the differences between the abuses and the effective uses of time-out. It is a book that explains to both parents and teachers the difference between positive uses of time-out that help children and humiliating uses of time-out. Although the humiliating time-outs may stop the behavior, they also hurt children.

The Long-Range Effects

ADULTS USE PUNITIVE time-out because they believe it will improve behavior. This is very shortsighted thinking.

Parents and teachers will not be effective until they realize that punitive time-out increases the very behavior they are trying to eliminate—or results in another misbehavior motivated by discouragement. Punitive time-out may stop the behavior for the moment, but it often creates further rebellion at best or loss of self-esteem at worst.

I wonder if anyone who uses time-out in a forceful, humiliating way ever thinks about the long-range effects on children. Parents and teachers who claim time-out is effective are defining *effective* only in terms of controlling the child and stopping the behavior for the moment. In this book, *effective* is defined only in terms of the long-range positive effects on the child. In other words, does the child feel encouraged and empowered? Will the child's behavior improve over the long run? Has the child learned an important life skill?

Positive Time-Out Is Only One Way to Encourage

POSITIVE TIME-OUT is not the only way to encourage and empower children. This book includes many other ways to avoid power struggles with children, all of which are designed to invite cooperation rather than foster resentment and rebellion. They all have a foundation in dignity and respect. They all teach children important life skills that will help them be successful, happy, contributing members of society. All of the methods discussed in this book achieve these important long-range results because of two criteria:

1. Children are involved respectfully whenever possible.

2. All methods incorporate kindness and firmness at the same time.

Please join me in the dream to eliminate punitive, humiliating time-out so we can empower children through the implementation of positive time-out and other methods of positive discipline.

Time-Out

Encouragement or Discouragement?

DURING MY LECTURES, I often ask audiences, "What is the most popular discipline method used today, besides spanking, yelling, threatening, bribery, and guilt?" The answers are always the same: time-out and the withdrawal of privileges. (We'll discuss withdrawal of privileges later in this chapter.)

These days *time-out* is a familiar concept to almost every parent and teacher: "I put my son in time-out until he can behave," one mother says. "I can't get my daughter to *stay* in time-out," wails another. A father laments, "It doesn't do any good to send my son to time-out; he enjoys it." A teacher complains that when he asks a student to step outside the classroom door until he can behave better, the student makes funny faces through the window. Other teachers complain that suspension (simply another form of punitive time-out) seems more like a reward for students than a punishment. (A whole book could be written about the implications of that statement! What does it say about the school environment or the discouragement of students when they see suspension as a reward?)

Defining Time-Out

WHAT EXACTLY IS time-out? To one frazzled mom, time-out means strapping her rebellious toddler in his high chair and setting an egg timer, one minute for each year of his age. In some schools, time-out means a segregated desk, a trip to the principal, isolation in a small room or booth, or suspension. For one terrified boy, time-out means standing for half an hour trying to press his nose against a circle drawn high on the wall by his frustrated father. And for some parents and teachers, time-out means time away from the group to "think about what you did!" Other popular terms for time-out include *grounding* and *detention*.

Can time-out really be all these things? Why is it such a popular discipline method? What should it be? First, let's discuss why time-out, in all its incarnations, is so popular. The rest of this book is dedicated to what time-out *can be* when used in a positive, rather than a negative, manner.

Beware of What Works!

PUNITIVE TIME-OUT is popular because it *seems* to work. I say "seems to work" because it does work if all you care about is stopping the behavior for the moment. However, it does not work if you are concerned about long-term results. For example, the isolation booth may *work* in that it stops misbehavior (after all, what can children do while locked up in a four-foot-square box?), but what are the long-range results for the children? What are they thinking, feeling, and deciding about themselves and about what to do in the future? Most adults are so enamored with the immediate, short-term results that they don't consider the long-term results. Isolation and humiliation may *work,* but they don't help children *feel* better so they can *do* better in the future.

FOUR Rs OF PUNISHMENT

1. Resentment: "This is unfair. I can't trust adults."
2. Revenge: "They're winning now, but I'll get even."
3. Rebellion: "I'll do just the opposite to prove that I don't have to do it their way."
4. Retreat into:
   a. Sneakiness: "I won't get caught next time."
   b. Reduced self-esteem: "I'm a bad person."

Many adults have been brainwashed with the idea that children have to suffer to learn. Children may learn while suffering punishment, but what exactly do they learn? The long-range results of punishment, as described in *Positive Discipline*

(Nelsen, 1996, 87–88), are that children may feel one or all of the Four Rs of Punishment (see box on page 3).

Short-range thinking related to misbehavior frequently incorporates punishment. Therefore, we need to look at long-

> Discipline that teaches children helps them *learn* for the future. Punishment makes children *pay* for the past.

term outcomes instead of short-term quick fixes that provide the *illusion* of effectiveness. Long-term parenting (and teaching) focuses on what children will learn that will help them long after the immediate crisis has passed. Discipline that teaches children helps them *learn* for the future. Punishment makes children *pay* for the past.

Punitive Time-Out: How Widespread? To What End?

WHEN I HEARD about the isolation booths used in some schools, I was outraged and sad. I tried to imagine the feelings of a child locked in a four-foot square booth with a window too high to see through. I thought, "Surely this practice must be limited to only a few schools." (I already knew time-out was overused and misused in too many homes.) Then I read an article that told of a boy confined all day for six weeks in a ten-foot by thirteen-foot isolation room in a Texas school. His crime? He had refused to cut his seven-inch ponytail. The article went on to report that this child now has nightmares about the walls of the classroom closing in and crushing him.

"But that's appalling," parents cry. "We would never do that to our children!" But is forcibly restraining a child in some time-out spot really all that different? What is our goal: to punish, to give ourselves a break from irritating behavior, or to help our children feel better because children who feel better, do better? Only positive time-out (discussed later in this chapter) accomplishes the latter.

Discipline and Punishment Are Not the Same

MANY PEOPLE BELIEVE that discipline and punishment are synonymous. They are not. Discipline comes from the Latin words *discipulus,* which means "pupil," and *disciplina,* which means "teaching" or "learning"—all very positive ideas. Punishment is not positive; it does not have long-range positive results for *any* human being. Adults use punitive time-out when they mistakenly believe that punishment is the best way to inspire improved behavior. But punitive time-out can be a nightmare for a child locked in a booth or other small space, powerless to get out or to change the situation until the amount of time determined by an adult has been served.

> Tactics that humiliate and deprive a child of dignity and respect are means that do not justify the end.

Adults who value basic human rights (especially for children) share this nightmare and believe tactics that humiliate and deprive a child of dignity and respect are means that do not justify the end.

The discipline of positive time-out can be used to teach. Children learn the value of taking time to cool off until they regain enough objectivity and perspective to use their wisdom and self-discipline. These life skills can serve them throughout their lives.

What or Who Is an Extremely Difficult Child?

ADVOCATES OF THE isolation booth say it is used only for extremely difficult children. But who defines "extremely difficult," and how does that label affect the child? Some teachers may define the slightest irritation as extremely difficult, while other teachers would not consider locking a child in an isolation booth no matter how severe the misbehavior. Some teachers have used the isolation booth for children who displayed the "extremely difficult" behavior of chewing gum or talking out of turn. Such ambiguous definitions are grounds for great concern.

Some teachers justify use of the isolation booth by saying children are given other options first, such as sitting at their desks with their heads down. If that doesn't work, they are asked to sit in a time-out area facing a three-sided box. If that doesn't work, they are locked in the isolation booth. The option they are *not* given is one that might help them feel encouraged and that might eliminate the misbehavior. This option is to calm down in a positive environment until they can rationally explore the consequences of their choices with a friendly adult who believes that mistakes are wonderful opportunities from which to learn.

Physical Abuse Isn't the Only Kind of Abuse

MANY ADULTS WHO don't believe in corporal punishment think it is okay to use time-out in a punitive, shaming way for their "difficult" or "defiant" child. They act as though punitive time-out will not be as damaging as physical abuse; however, a damaged ego (emotional abuse) can be just as harmful and difficult for children to deal with as physical abuse is.

It can be tremendously frustrating to deal with misbehaving children, whether at home or in school. The incidence of violence in our schools is rising almost daily. We hear more and more about the difficult or the defiant child. But where does defiance begin? Could it be that parents and teachers have the cart before the horse? Could it be that any kind of punishment helps create "difficult" or "defiant" children? Is it possible that "difficult" or "defiant" children are very intelligent with a low tolerance for being overly controlled and disrespectfully treated? Whatever the case, confining children to small spaces is a disturbing practice, and it increases the discouragement that is at the root of all misbehavior. Adults who send children to punitive time-out perpetuate a vicious cycle.

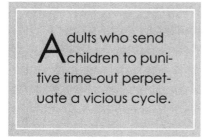

Adults who send children to punitive time-out perpetuate a vicious cycle.

Be Rational

MANY PARENTS AND teachers say ridiculous things, such as "Go to your room (or to the corner) and think about what you did." I'm amazed that many adults don't know the answer when I ask, "Do you know why that is a ridiculous statement?" They come up with all kinds of responses such as, "The child might be too angry to think about it." "He might fall asleep." "She might not understand what she did wrong." All of these statements are true, but what is ridiculous is the assumption that adults can control what a child thinks. Parents and teachers look chagrined when I ask, "Do you really think you can control what a child thinks?"

I go on to ask, "What do you think the child is really thinking about?" The answers range from "She is probably thinking about how angry at me she is," to "She is thinking about how to avoid getting caught next time," to "She may be thinking about how to get even with me," to, worst of all, "She may be thinking she is a bad person." Although all of these an-swers are probably true of the child, none helps a child do bet-ter in the future.

> Punitive time-out is based on the silly thought that to get children to do better, we first have to make them feel worse. Positive time-out is based on the understanding that children do better when they feel better.

Most adults do not realize that children are constantly making decisions about themselves, about their world, and, based on those decisions, about what to do to survive or to thrive. (The four categories of decisions that children make are covered in Chapter 5.)

Punitive time-out is based on the silly thought that to get children to do better, we first have to make them feel worse. Positive time-out is based on the understanding that children do better when they feel better. Think about these ideas in terms of yourself. Do you do better when you feel worse, or when you feel better? Punitive time-out is certainly not effec-tive if it perpetuates children's discouraging beliefs about them-selves and their environment. Nor is it effective if those beliefs increase the need for revenge or rebellion in whatever form it takes.

What Does *Effective* Mean?

ANOTHER TERM THAT needs closer examination is *effective*. Some teachers and psychologists believe that the isolation booth is effective. But effective for what and for whom? Effective for the parent or teacher or for the child?

During Positive Discipline workshops, we do many experimental activities designed to help people "get into the child's world" to understand the long-range effects of our discipline methods. At these workshops, we have people imagine, or role-play, that they are young children of any age confined to a small space, strapped in a high chair, or otherwise humiliated or isolated. Most people said they felt scared, abandoned, powerless, shamed, and insecure about their basic worth as people. When we did the same exercise with adults role-playing older children in the same situation, the adults felt humiliated, angry, and revengeful; they thought about dropping out of school or about how to get even with those who had shamed them. Even worse were those who felt (while role-playing children in punitive time-out), "I'm not a very good person. I'm nothing but a disappointment to my parents or teachers. I'll never be good enough."

Imagine that you are a child of any age. Imagine now what you would feel being sent to punitive time-out. Would the experience encourage you to do better? Or would it crush your self-esteem, make you feel bad and inferior, or give you incentive for revenge? The healthiest response we have received from adults who have tried this exercise is, "It would give me something to brag about . . . that the only way they could control me is to lock me up." Not one adult has ever said, "I really felt this was good for me and provided me with an inner motivation to do better." Some have said, "I might do better out of total fear and at great cost to my self-esteem."

You may be thinking, "Surely making my child stay in his room for five minutes isn't that bad." The answer depends on the belief behind the act: Are you giving your child a chance to feel better and behave more constructively? Or are you simply interested in controlling your child's behavior? What is really going on in the mind of your child? Is your use of time-out effective in terms of long-range results?

The Effectiveness of Positive Time-Out

POSITIVE TIME-OUT can help children learn many important life skills, such as the importance of taking time to calm down until they can think more clearly and act more thoughtfully. When human beings are upset, they function from their primitive brain (the brain stem) where the only options are fight or flight. When adults send children to time-out, the adults are often functioning from their primitive brain, and resentment puts children in their primitive brain—perpetuating the vicious cycle of fight or flight.

Positive time-out allows children (and adults) to calm down until they are again functioning from their rational brain

(their cortex)—so they can solve problems and learn. Positive time-out encourages children to form positive beliefs about themselves, their world, and their behavior. In this state of mind, they can learn from their mistakes and/or determine how to make amends for any hurt or damage their behavior might have caused.

Be Aware of What Really Works

IF A METHOD has really worked with children, then it should make the children feel empowered and motivated to improve from an inner locus of control and desire to change (as opposed to control from others). Children should develop skills that will help them solve problems and improve behavior.

"Where did we ever get the crazy idea that to make children do better, we must first make them feel worse?" Let it be stated again: Children do better when they feel better, not when they are discouraged about themselves. Therefore, the number one criterion for positive time-out is that it be used to help children feel better, not to make them feel worse.

By understanding a few basic principles of human behavior, adults can empower children (see box on page 12).

Summary

POSITIVE TIME-OUT gives misbehaving, discouraged children, and adults, time to cool off, feel better, and change disruptive behavior to constructive behavior. It can be an affirming, loving action that demonstrates faith in a child's ability to gain control and solve problems. Taking time to calm down until inner wisdom can be accessed is an important life skill—one that would benefit many adults as well as children. Positive time-out can be very effective because *children do better when they feel better*—an idea that is repeated many times throughout this book.

Our motives and goals in dealing with the children entrusted to our care need to be examined. The goal of positive time-out, as with everything we do as parents and teachers, should be to help our children grow into capable, respectful, cooperative people with many social and life skills. The criteria for reaching this goal are covered in Chapter 2.

BASIC PRINCIPLES OF HUMAN BEHAVIOR

1. All people (including children) deserve dignity and respect. This is a basic principle of Adlerian psychology—the philosophy of maintaining dignity and respect for all human beings. The idea must be incorporated before time-out can be used as an effective, encouraging experience that helps children, instead of an experience that creates humiliation and loss of dignity and respect.

2. Misbehaving children are discouraged children. Misbehaving children need encouragement so they won't feel the need to misbehave. Shame and humiliation will only make them feel more discouraged and more motivated to misbehave. (Chapter 5 provides further details on this principle as well as the Four Mistaken Goals of Behavior and how they relate to time-out.)

3. Humiliation and shame are not effective motivators. During the past decade, a number of professionals concerned with children (pediatricians, psychiatrists, social workers, and so on) have formally adopted positions in opposition to spanking, paddling, or humiliating children in any way. These specialists have paid attention to the research demonstrating that the long-range damage to children far outweighs the immediate advantage of controlling behavior through punishment.

2

If Not Punitive Time-Out, Then What?

Parents and teachers often tell me they have tried everything to deal with a misbehaving child, and nothing works. When I ask them to list everything they have tried, everything on their list is punitive. Why is it so difficult for adults to give up punishment when they experience over and over that it doesn't work? Answer: They fear that the only alternative is permissiveness. Positive time-out is not permissive, nor are any of the other nonpunitive methods suggested in this book.

Before adults can convey the benefits of positive time-out, they have to get rid of their old ideas about punitive time-out. Some ways to do this are to think of time-out in new ways.

The Sports Analogy

ADULTS AND SCHOOL-AGE children can comprehend the idea of time-out in sports, where the purpose is to stop the clock, catch your breath, regroup, take a look at what isn't working, and come up with a new plan. Positive time-out can do the same for both children and adults. It can stop the clock on negative behavior and allow time for calming down before new behavior is possible. Since children do better when they feel better, they will be able to regroup and come up with a new plan that will serve them and others.

CRITERIA FOR POSITIVE TIME-OUT

1. Positive time-out is designed to encourage children and to teach them self-control and self-discipline.

2. Positive time-out is respectful because children are involved participants rather than objects or victims of the process.

3. Positive time-out teaches children to understand that their brains don't function well when they are upset. They learn the value of taking time to calm down until their brains are functioning in a way that is advantageous, rather than detrimental, to them.

Time-Out on Grandma's Lap

KATE TALUGA, OF Tallahassee, Florida, thought of a marvelous way to convey the vision of time-out as an encouraging, nurturing place for children to go. She created a life-size "Grandma." Grandma had a big foam cushion for a lap and a large bosom stuffed with soft cotton. She also wore an apron with pockets full of books and small stuffed animals. When children need time-out, they go sit on Grandma's lap. Kate takes her "Grandma" to child-care centers and introduces her to the children as she teaches them about positive time-out.

Self-Soothing

A NURTURING ENVIRONMENT helps children in the process of self-soothing. What does *self-soothing* mean? When you feel anxious, self-soothing is the ability to come back to your center until you feel better. Sometimes it means learning to tolerate frustration or discomfort until it passes. It may mean knowing that there are things you can do (such as take timeout) to ease the discomfort until it does pass. There are many degrees of anxiety, and some degrees take less time for self-soothing than others.

Anxiety is a normal component of living. We get anxious when we are scared, when we don't get what we want, when we feel rejected, when we feel hurt, when we feel powerless. The list could go on and on. The good news is that we are born with several coping, or self-soothing, abilities, and as we grow we can learn other coping skills. The bad news is that many parents and teachers think "good" parenting and teaching means extinguishing children's self-soothing abilities instead of allowing them to develop. These same parents and teachers avoid teaching additional self-soothing skills, often because they are too busy fixing every problem children encounter or using punishment instead of helping children manage their own behavior. What they often do not understand is that positive time-out provides children the opportunity to enhance their innate ability to self-soothe instead of having that ability extinguished by adults who overprotect or punish.

Positive time-out provides children the opportunity to enhance their innate ability to self-soothe instead of having that ability extinguished by adults who overprotect or punish.

Inherent Abilities to Self-Soothe

TRONICK AND GIANINO (1986) researched infants' ability to self-soothe and discovered that infants self-soothe several times in a minute. If you observe an infant, you will notice what Tronick and Gianino discovered. Infants will stare at a person or object intently for several seconds. Then they will look away to self-center before returning to stare at the same object or focusing on something else. In other words, the infants take a little time-out.

Alone Time

CHILDREN NEED SOME alone time to maintain their inherent self-soothing ability. Too many parents think that children need to be constantly entertained or comforted. If adults can't provide the entertainment or comfort personally, they provide mobiles, jumpers, automatic swings. This does not mean that infants should never have a mobile. It does mean, however, that parents might provide more balance between stimulation and alone time if they respected the innate ability to self-soothe. They might feel less guilty about allowing an infant to play alone with her toes (or even a rattle) instead of thinking she needs constant stimulation. They might realize that a little fussing might simply be part of the self-soothing process.

Again, I'm not saying that infants should never have stimulation or comfort from adults. Research has demonstrated the importance of talking to infants, playing with them, providing interesting objects for them to look at and play with. The problem is that we adults have a tendency to overdo. When is crying an attempt to communicate a need, and when is it an expression of mild anxiety that would be best served through self-soothing? When we don't allow children to practice and enhance their inherent ability to self-soothe, do we teach them instead to develop the habit of demanding comfort from others? Understanding the benefits of self-soothing may inspire parents to find a balance among time for self-soothing, stimulation, and comfort. It may also increase their understanding of the benefits of positive time-out.

Getting Children Involved in Creating a Positive Time-Out Area

ONCE ADULTS UNDERSTAND the value of positive time-out, they can start teaching it to children. The best way to get children involved is to let them help create the positive time-out area. This involvement is the key to building children's respect and empowerment. Children are motivated to follow a plan when they have been respectfully involved in its creation. The following four steps are key to getting a child involved in the process:

INVOLVING CHILDREN IN THE CREATION OF A POSITIVE TIME-OUT AREA

1. Discuss the purpose of positive time-out.

2. Let children create a name for the positive time-out area.

3. Let children help design the positive time-out area.

4. Establish rules for the use of positive time-out.

Discuss the Purpose of Positive Time-Out

POSITIVE TIME-OUT can—and should—be discussed with children of all ages before it is actually needed. However, as you will read in Chapter 3, positive time-out for children below the age of reason is rarely effective.

When everyone feels calm, explain to your children or students that all of us—parents, teachers, and children alike—have times when we lose control of our behavior, feel upset, or find ourselves in a bad mood. This doesn't mean we *are* bad; it just means that we feel too bad to know what kind of behavior would help others and us. During these times, it can be helpful to have a time-out place to sit quietly and wait until we feel better. This is not a time to sit and think about how bad we are, to do work, to write sentences, or to do anything else that could be considered punishing or humiliating. This is a time to do whatever we need to feel better and to know that the upset feelings or bad mood will pass. Sometimes it helps just to let ourselves feel what we feel—and even to look for the wisdom in our feelings. Some people find it helpful to ask themselves, "What are these feelings trying to teach me?" Sometimes it is

helpful to think happy thoughts or to do something distracting such as reading a good book, listening to music, or taking a nap.

Involve children in the conversation by asking, "When do you feel like doing good things—when you feel bad or when you feel good?" Lead them in a discussion of why they might not feel like doing good when they feel bad: they are angry, mad, upset, can't think straight, and so on. (You might want discuss the idea of fight or flight, as described in Chapters 1 and 8.)

Let children know that when they go to positive time-out, *they* can decide when they feel good enough to behave in ways that will be helpful to them and to others.

Ask children if they have noticed that something often seems better after they have had time to calm down? Ask for ideas about why a cooling-off place (positive time-out area) might help people.

Let children know you are going to work together to create a positive time-out area where they can go when they feel bad or upset—a place that will help them feel better. Let children know that when they go to positive time-out, *they* can decide when they feel good enough to behave in ways that will be helpful to them and to others.

Let Children Create a Name for the Positive Time-Out Area

I CONTINUE TO use the word *time-out* because I'm trying to change the way people think about it. However, because time-out has such negative connotations, it may be helpful for children to call the time-out area something that will help them remember the positive purpose of time-out. Some examples of names that children have chosen include the Cooling-Off Place, the Feel-Better Place, the Quiet-Time Spot, the Feel Better-Do Better Place, the Back-to-Sanity Place, the Self-Control Helper, or even Hawaii. Letting children create a name increases not only their understanding of positive time-out but also their ownership of it.

Have children brainstorm what they think would be a good name for the positive time-out area. Keep track of their ideas on a flip chart or a large piece of paper. Children can then vote on one name, or each child can call it whatever he or she wants—as long as the name conveys the positive meanings of time-out.

Let Children Help Design the Positive Time-Out Area

ONCE CHILDREN HAVE chosen a name, brainstorm with them what should go in the positive time-out area. Include things that might help children calm down and feel better. The list usually includes stuffed animals, books, soft pillows or

beanbags, headphones and a CD player for soft music. It might also include paper and crayons for drawing about feelings or for journaling (not for writing sentences required by the parent or teacher). Some children like to include a punching bag to express their anger.

Once all the ideas are listed, let the children circle the items they want to include and eliminate the rest. (In classrooms, ask children to eliminate items that are not respectful and practical, such as loud music, candy, live animals, a massage therapist, and so on.)

One school class decided to have teddy bears and pillows in the time-out area. They also decided that each child would take responsibility for deciding when he or she felt better and was ready to rejoin the class. A kitchen timer was provided for those who wanted to make a guess about how much time they would need.

Another class decided to have notebooks in the time-out area so they could write about their feelings if they felt like it. The teacher of this class had taught the journaling process, and these children had learned that writing journal style gave them a perspective they didn't have before.

One youngster kept a cozy corner of her room stocked with favorite books, stuffed animals, and a tape recorder with music.

W hen children understand that we can all feel discouraged at times and that they can determine when they are ready to change their behavior, they will feel encouraged.

Going to the time-out corner was an opportunity for her to have a few moments with things she knew would help her feel better. She sometimes chose to stay there quite contentedly!

When children understand that we can all feel discouraged at times and that they can determine when they are ready to change their behavior, they will feel encouraged, which is the basis of belonging and significance.

Establish Rules for the Use of Positive Time-Out

SOME TEACHERS ARE afraid students will misuse positive time-out. When positive time-out is created in the appropriate atmosphere, however, this misuse usually doesn't happen. To ease your mind, however, it is okay to have students create rules for positive time-out. Start by asking them, "What guidelines do we need to be sure that people don't misuse the positive time-out area?" Children usually come up with the same guidelines teachers might impose, such as only one person at a time, no longer than ten minutes, no more than twice a day.

Other teachers trust the process and have found that students don't misuse positive time-out when they have been respectfully involved in the process. Several teachers allow their students to stay in positive time-out for as long as they feel they need it. (These teachers know that most students don't choose isolation unless they are extremely discouraged; and this would be a clue that something else needs to be done.)

A Time-Out Buddy

MANY TEACHERS ALLOW students to take a time-out buddy with them. Some teachers have taught time-out buddy listening skills. The buddies are taught to listen and empathize, but to avoid giving advice.

Positive Time-Out in High Schools

I WAS DOUBTFUL that positive time-out would work in high schools until I saw what a tenth-grade class created: Hawaii. They built a palm tree, painted a mural of sand and sea, brought in plush sea animals such as seals, dolphins, whales, and sea lions, and set up beach chairs. Even though "Hawaii" looked like the most appealing place in the room, the teacher claimed that her students did not misuse it by spending all their time there. This could be because part of their planning included establishing rules for the use of the positive time-out area.

The Positive Time-Out Bench

THE TIME-OUT BENCH is used for outdoor positive time-out, such as on a school playground. Some schools that use a time-out bench in a positive way call it the Happy Bench or the Feel-Good Bench. When children misbehave on the playground, they are invited to sit on the Happy Bench until they have calmed down and feel ready to behave respectfully. If the request is made in a punitive tone, it will not be effective. A friendly, respectful tone of voice is imperative. Effectiveness is increased when time-out is one of two or more choices, "Which would help you the most right now, to take some positive time-out or to put this problem on the class-meeting agenda?" (Parents can offer a choice between positive time-out and the family-meeting agenda.)

Adults and Positive Time-Out

MANY PARENTS AND teachers find it difficult to change their old habits of using time-out in a punitive manner. The following guidelines may be helpful.

ADULT GUIDELINES FOR POSITIVE TIME-OUT

1. Positive time-out is not the only effective discipline tool.

2. Allow children to choose positive time-out.

3. It is okay to suggest positive time-out.

4. Let children decide how much time-out they need.

Positive Time-Out Is Not the Only Effective Discipline Tool

THE FIRST GUIDELINE is to remember that positive time-out is not the only discipline tool available. It is not appropriate for every behavior, with every child, all the time. (Many other discipline tools are suggested throughout this book and in other *Positive Discipline* books.)

Allow Children to Choose Positive Time-Out

POSITIVE TIME-OUT IS most effective if children choose to go there, which is likely if they have been involved in the creation process. Let children know that they can go to positive time-out whenever they feel the need. Let them know you might go to your own positive time-out when you need it.

Children feel empowered when they have a choice. They don't have to lose face; they can use their power to choose.

It Is Okay to Suggest Positive Time-Out

WHEN CHILDREN DON'T think to choose positive time-out, you might suggest, "Do you think it would help you to go to the positive time-out area now?" Place emphasis on the words "help you." If they say no, you might suggest, "Would it help you if I went to positive time-out with you?" (Teachers can also suggest, "Would you like to take a time-out buddy with you?") If they still say no, you might say, "Well, I think I will go. I think it will help me." There are at least three benefits when you choose to go to positive time-out yourself:

1. It is great modeling for your children or students.
2. It could be that you are the one who needs time-out the most.
3. It is an excellent way to defuse a power struggle, which requires at least two people.

Some teachers have asked for a volunteer (or even another student) to take over the class while he or she goes to the time-out area in the classroom.

Let Children Decide How Much Time-Out They Need

SOME CHILDREN ENJOY having a timer in the positive time-out area. Instead of adults demanding that children stay in time-out for a certain amount of time, children are invited to set the timer to the amount of time they think they might need to feel better. Allowing children the choice to decide when they are ready to come out of time-out is extremely important for increasing their sense of accountability, responsibility, and autonomy. They are empowered with a sense of self-control and self-discipline. Many adults miss this point and set themselves up for unnecessary power struggles when they force children into time-out, try to make them feel

> Allowing children the choice to decide when they are ready to come out of time-out is extremely important for increasing their sense of accountability, responsibility, and autonomy.

ashamed, and exert control over when children can leave time-out. Everyone is unique. Some people can feel better after a few minutes of positive time-out. Others will need more time.

When time-out is structured in a positive way, children can recognize its value. Many children take responsibility to go there on their own when they need it. Some may need a gentle reminder, such as "Do you think you can behave respectfully, or do you think you need to go to time-out until you feel better?" Tone of voice and body language are the key factors that determine if children will see time-out as a helpful or a punitive experience.

Must Time-Out Always Be the Child's Choice?

THERE ARE EXCEPTIONS to every rule. Even though positive time-out is most effective when children choose it, there are times when children can still learn even though sending them to time-out is the parent or teacher's choice.

Three-year-old Melissa would constantly bop her one-year-old brother, Dee, on the head. She started to think this was funny and began boasting, "I hit Dee." Her mother tried jumping into the fray to show Melissa how to touch Dee nicely. However, the bopping on the head increased.

Finally Mom got Melissa to help design a positive time-out area in her room. Melissa chose to have a beanbag and her favorite teddy bear in her Favorite Place. Then Mom informed Melissa that she had faith in her to treat Dee nicely and that if Melissa forgot, she could go to her Favorite Place until she remembered to treat her brother kindly. For the next few weeks, every time Melissa hit Dee, Mom would scoop her up (kindly and firmly) and take Melissa to her Favorite Place. Mom didn't scold or say a word while doing this.

When Melissa would appear back in the living room, Mom would say, "I'm glad you are feeling better. Would you like to show me how you can touch Dee tenderly?" Melissa would go over and pat Dee's arm or give him a nice hug. In about three weeks, the hitting diminished considerably and Melissa became more considerate with her little brother.

It was effective for Mom to put Melissa in positive time-out for three reasons:

1. Melissa helped create her time-out area (her Favorite Place).

2. Mom was kind and firm while taking Melissa to time-out.

3. Mom followed through by asking Melissa to make amends through respectful behavior.

Following Through After Positive Time-Out

MANY PEOPLE OBJECt that positive time-out is a reward for misbehavior. They think children are being allowed to do something pleasant after misbehaving. When you understand that a misbehaving child is a discouraged child (discussed in more detail in Chapter 5), you will see that this is not true. It is very wise to take time to cool off rather than immediately acting irrationally. The most effective way to deal with misbehavior is to help children feel encouraged so their motive for misbehaving is removed.

Often positive time-out is enough to change the behavior—and isn't that the point? As discussed before, some adults don't realize that they are more interested in making children pay for what they did than they are in helping them change their behavior for the future.

One mother shared that she sent her two-year-old to time-out for misbehavior. He toddled out in a few seconds. Mom proudly reported that she "put him right back." I asked, "Was he still misbehaving when he came out of time-out in a few seconds?" She admitted he wasn't. I asked, "Then why did you put him back in time-out? Was your purpose to help him change his behavior or to make him pay for his old behavior?" She admitted, "I never really thought about it. I guess I always thought punishment would change his behavior. I can see that I wasn't really thinking about the results of what I was doing."

Other times it is wise to follow up after positive time-out by helping children who can talk explore and learn from their behavior. This means waiting until the child feels better and is in a state of mind where you can discuss what happened and what needs to be done.

Sometimes children need to make amends when their behavior has been hurtful or destructive. However, it is useless to require this when they are still upset and might make amends just because they feel forced. When they have had time to calm down and feel better, they are more willing to explore ways to make amends or simply to demonstrate respectful behavior. After positive time-out, adults can help children explore the benefits of making amends so children do it by choice. Brainstorm with your child about how to fix what has been broken or how to help someone feel better if they have been hurt. Sharing their ideas about how to make amends is very empowering to children.

Time-Out Works for Adults, Too!

YOU MAY BE thinking that this sort of time-out would *never* work for your child. But it might—if your children can see how well it works for you. Parents can model using time-out with dignity and respect.

Barbara's nine-year-old son had come home an hour late; dinner was cold, and what was worse, Barbara had been worried sick. When Rick finally appeared, looking both defiant and guilty, Barbara realized that, at that moment, anger had the upper hand. So she said to her son, "Rick, I'm glad you're okay—I've been worried. But right now I'm so upset that I need to take time-out to calm down before we discuss what has happened."

Later, when Barbara felt more relaxed (and when both she and Rick had a chance to think about what would happen next), she sat down with her son to find out what had happened, what had caused it, and what ideas each of them had for resolving the problem. (See more about asking what and how questions in Chapters 4 and 10.) Although it took awhile to come to an agreement, the episode ended with a hug and a smile, and both Barbara and Rick felt good about each other.

If Barbara had followed her initial reaction, she would have punished Rick for his disobedience and, perhaps, never have

Children learn positive, long-range lessons of responsibility and self-discipline when they feel encouraged, when they feel belonging and significance, and when they feel they have some power over their lives. Positive time-out provides opportunities for children to develop these feelings.

learned what had really happened. By taking time-out, she calmed down and remembered several problem-solving tips from her parenting class:

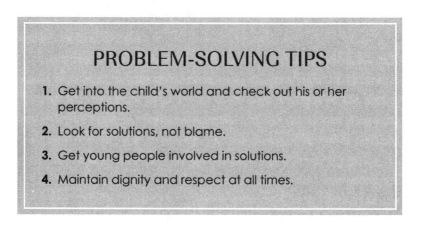

PROBLEM-SOLVING TIPS

1. Get into the child's world and check out his or her perceptions.
2. Look for solutions, not blame.
3. Get young people involved in solutions.
4. Maintain dignity and respect at all times.

A Panacea . . . Not!

POSITIVE TIME-OUT IS not a panacea and is not appropriate for every circumstance. (In Chapter 3 I discuss why positive time-out is usually not effective for children under the age of three.) Later in the book, we will explore many other positive discipline tools as well as different ways to use positive time-out. For example, instead of time-out, a family or class may decide to put a problem on the family- or class-meeting agenda, which allows for some cooling-off time before a problem is discussed.

Meanwhile, try positive time-out. You'll love it—and so will your children.

3

Time-Out for Children Under the Age of Reason

C HILDREN UNDER THE age of two-and-a-half should not be sent to time-out unless they choose it, which may be very rare, or unless an adult goes with them. There are, of course, exceptions to most rules. One mother approached me after a lecture and shared how she successfully used positive time-out with her eighteen-month-old child. She said her son, Jason, had a satin pillow that he liked very much. He seemed to find this pillow very soothing. When Jason seemed cranky, she would say to him, "Would you like to lie on your comfy pillow for awhile?" Sometimes he would just go to his pillow and lie down until he felt better. If he hesitated, she would ask, "Do you want me to go with you?" When he wanted her to go with him, they would just snuggle for awhile, or they would look at one of his picture books. Soon he would be ready to return to exploring his world.

This mother had the attitude and understanding required to make positive time-out work with a child who has not reached the age of reason (or any child, for that matter). She understood child development enough to know that Jason was not misbehaving. Even though a misbehaving child is usually a discouraged child (see Chapter 5), for toddlers it is usually something else. Often their misbehavior stems from tiredness or from frustration at their lack of skills for getting what they want or need. They often feel confused and rebellious when parents or teachers don't understand their developmental need to explore and experiment. (See *Positive Discipline: The First Three Years* [Nelsen, Erwin, and Duffy, 1998] for more information on developmental needs.) Jason's mother's attitude was one of loving gentleness, patience, kindness, and firmness. She was firm in her knowledge that Jason's behavior was socially unpleasant and frustrating to him and that something needed to be done about it. She was kind in her method of helping him deal with it.

What or When Is the Age of Reason?

WEBSTER'S DICTIONARY DEFINES the *age of reason* as "the time of life when one begins to be able to distinguish right from wrong." This definition sounds simple enough until you start to examine it. My first question is, "Begins to distinguish, or does distinguish?" Then I ask, "When does this age begin? Why do some adults still do unreasonable things if they have reached the age of reason? What other factors are involved? What about brain development, moral development, outside influences, self-control, and on and on?" The one thing I do know is that toddlers (and even older children) do not have the reasoning ability many adults seem to think they have.

What Does Your Child Under Three Really "Know" About "No"?

CHILDREN UNDER THE age of three do not understand "no" in the way most parents think they do. (And a full understanding of no doesn't occur magically when the child turns three; it is a developmental process.) *No* is an abstract concept that is in direct opposition to the developmental need of young children to explore their world and to develop their sense of autonomy (as discussed in Chapter 7 of *Positive Discipline: The First Three Years* [Nelsen, Erwin, and Duffy, 1998]) and their sense of initiative (as discussed in Chapter 4 of *Positive Discipline for Preschoolers* [Nelsen, Erwin, and Duffy, 1998]).

Oh, your child may know at some level that you don't want her to do something. She may even know she will get an angry reaction from you if she does it. However, she cannot understand *why* in the way an adult thinks she can. Why else would a child look at you before doing what she knows she shouldn't do, grin engagingly, and do it anyway? Knowing things as a toddler means something far different from knowing things as an adult. Her version of knowing lacks the internal controls necessary to halt her roving fingers.

Understanding Developmental and Age Appropriateness

AROUND THE AGES of one through three, children enter the "me do it" stage—the stage when they develop a sense of autonomy or of doubt and shame. This means it is a child's developmental job to explore and experiment. Can you imagine how confusing it is to a child to be punished for what he is developmentally programmed to do? He is faced with a real dilemma (at a subconscious level): "Do I obey my parents, or do I follow my biological drive to develop autonomy and skills by exploring and experimenting in my world?"

> Can you imagine how confusing it is to a child to be punished for what he is developmentally programmed to do?

Brain (Intellectual) Development

SWISS DEVELOPMENTALIST Jean Piaget discovered that toddlers lack the ability to understand cause and effect. In fact, higher-order thinking like understanding consequences and ethics may not develop until children are as old as ten. Therefore, it does not make sense for adults to use negative time-out or any other punitive method because children may not have the ability to reason why they are in time-out. Positive time-out, however, helps children feel better so they do better. It doesn't require reasoning.

Piaget engaged children in many experimental activities to discover their intellectual development. I repeated several of these activities as demonstrations while teaching child development at a community college. Two of my favorites I call "Glasses of Water" and "Balls of Clay."

I would ask a student to bring a three-year-old and a six-year-old child to the classroom. A student would wait outside the classroom with the six-year-old while I first demonstrated with the three-year-old as follows. Two drinking glasses of exactly the same size were filled with exactly the same amount of water. I asked the three-year-old if she could see that the glasses had the same amount of water. After she agreed, I would ask her to watch closely while I poured one of the glasses of water into an empty, short, fat glass and the other into an empty, tall, thin glass. When this was completed, I would ask, "Do each of these glasses (the tall, thin one and the short, fat one) have the same amount of water now?" The three-year-old always insisted that they did not—the tall, thin glass had more water. Even when I pointed out, again, that I had poured the same amount of water into the tall, thin glass as I had into the short, fat glass, I could never convince a three-year-old that both glasses had the same amount of water. Does this mean the three-year-olds were stupid? Of course not. This experiment only verified, over and over, that three-year-olds (and younger children, and children a little older) did not yet have the brain development to reason in this manner. Piaget called this inability the "lack of the ability to conserve."

When I repeated the same demonstration with six-year-olds, they always knew that the tall, thin glass and the short, fat glass had the same amount of water after being poured from identical glasses. (One six-year-old child pointed out to me that they didn't have the same amount of water because I spilled a few drops while pouring from one container to the other.) Somewhere between the ages of four to six (not the same for every child), children develop the ability to conserve.

For the other demonstration, I took two balls of clay that were exactly the same size. After the children agreed they were the same, I would squash one flat (right in front of the children) and then ask if they were still the same. The three-year-olds always thought one was bigger than the other was, while the six-year-olds always knew they were still the same.

Implications of Intellectual Development

HOW COULD IT possibly make sense to use punitive time-out (or any punishment, for that matter) with young children? (We have already discussed why punishment may not be effective with older children.) I'm sure adults use punishment with children because they think it will improve the behavior of the children. And, as pointed out earlier, it may, but only for the short term. However, very young children do not make the connection between the "crime" and the "punishment" that adults assume they will. For example, parents almost always cite the danger of a child running into the street as a justification for spanking a toddler. Reasons include the life-and-death nature of the situation, the need for immediate compliance, and the effectiveness of a spanking for "getting a child's attention." The thing adults forget is that to a toddler, an angry, shouting, spanking parent is probably far more frightening than any street. After receiving punishment for running in the street, a child may be in more danger of being hit by a car because instead of watching for cars, she is watching to see if her parents are going to punish her.

I always ask parents who believe spanking will teach their child to stay out of the street, "After you have spanked your two-year-old, will you now let her play in front of a busy street unsupervised?" They say, "No, but she sure doesn't run into the street when I'm around." "Right," I reply, "But, what about when you are not around? How many times do you have to spank her before you think it is safe to leave her unsupervised near a busy street?" They admit that they wouldn't let her play unsupervised until she reaches the age of six or seven. I rest my case. If supervision is required (and that is a parent's job), why not use kind and firm methods of supervision, such as teaching children to look both ways to see if any cars are coming and to decide when they think it is safe? Then, by the time they are old enough to be on their own, they will have skills rather than fear or sneakiness.

Permissiveness . . . Not

THE STAGES OF intellectual and social development do not mean children should be allowed to do anything they want. The stages do explain why all methods to gain cooperation should be simultaneously kind and firm rather than shaming and/or punitive. This is a time in life when children's personalities are being formed, and they need an environment where they can make decisions about themselves that say, "I am competent. I can try, make mistakes, and learn. I am loved. I am a good person." If a child learns by guilt, shame, and punishment, that child is more likely to decide, "I'm not good, I'm not capable, and I'd better not take risks" or "I'd better be careful to avoid getting caught if I make a mistake."

Until children complete their intellectual development, which is an ongoing process that even some adults have not fully mastered, it does not make sense to expect children to learn positive things from punitive time-out.

Supervision, Distraction, Redirection

MANY EFFECTIVE DISCIPLINE tools other than positive time-out are presented in this book. Let's start at the very beginning, with the primary discipline tools for children under the age of reason. Young children need constant supervision along with distraction and/or redirection. This means removal, kindly and firmly, from what they can't do and guidance to an activity they can do. Remember, children under the age of three can't understand the reasoning behind punishment. If they can't understand reasoning, why try to reason? But punishment is not the answer either. Although it may stop the behavior for the moment, what long-range messages are children receiving? Are they deciding, "I'm bad. I'll get even and hurt back. I'll hit others when I'm bigger. Yelling at people is a good way to communicate. I won't get caught next time."? Children aren't consciously aware of the decisions they are making, but they are making decisions nonetheless. (More about this is in Chapter 5.)

> Young children need constant supervision along with distraction and/or redirection. This means removal, kindly and firmly, from what they can't do and guidance to an activity they can do.

It is almost funny when parents complain that they don't want to have to constantly supervise their young children. What do they think parenting is about? Even funnier (I'm not sure that is the best word) is when parents complain about having to use distraction and redirection over and over. It is funny because these same parents use punishment over and over, which is just as time consuming and a lot less fun—to say nothing of the damage it does to children.

It is so important to remember that parents need many different parenting skills and tools. There is never one tool (or three or even ten) that is effective for every situation and for every child. Sometimes positive time-out is effective for children over the age of three, and many times something else would work better. This is why many suggestions are provided in this book and in *Positive Discipline A–Z* (Nelsen, Lott, and Glenn, 1999).

It can be very valuable for adults to learn about developmental and age-appropriate behavior so their expectations do not go beyond the developmental capability of a child. Meanwhile, before the age of two-and-a-half, adults should go to time-out *with* the child. Adults can approach children with something like, "Let's take some time-out to read a book or listen to music until we feel better." In this way adults model the purpose of positive time-out, so it will be a familiar process by the time the child is developmentally ready to use it.

4

Punishment and Rewards Are Not Effective Long-Term Motivators

SOME PARENTS AND teachers believe that sending children to time-out with instructions to do something to help them feel better is rewarding their misbehavior. These adults believe that children need to suffer and feel bad before they will change their behavior. "Change their behavior to what?" we might ask. "To be responsible" is one of the most popular replies.

What Is Responsibility?

"HOW WOULD YOU describe a child who is responsible?" When adults are asked that question, they usually reply, "A child who does what he is supposed to do—a good child." But this is not what it means to be responsible. Response-ability means just that—the ability to respond.

Would you be willing to be responsible if by doing so you experience blame, shame, or pain? Children learn responsibility only in a safe environment. Punishment does not create a safe environment. And neither punishment nor rewards helps children develop responsibility.

> True learning takes place when children have the ability to respond to their experiences with important life skills, such as accountability, learning from mistakes, problem-solving, and understanding the consequences of their choices—to themselves and to others.

Who Learns Responsibility from Punishment and Rewards?

PUNISHMENT AND REWARDS teach adults, not children, to be responsible. Think about any program or method that involves rewards and punishment. It's an adult's job to catch kids being *good* and give them rewards and to catch them being *bad* and mete out punishment. What happens when the adult is no longer around?

Considerable research has demonstrated that children who experience an external locus of control don't develop responsibility, self-discipline, self-control, or any of the other behaviors that help children lead happy, contributing lives. In fact, a heavy-handed approach to teaching children how to behave is not only less effective but also more likely to be associated with disruptive and aggressive behavior patterns when the child is away from home. The problem is that most of this research is buried in academic journals.

The volumes of research presented in Alfie Kohn's book, *Punished by Rewards* (1993), demonstrate the long-range destructive results of punishment and rewards. This book is highly recommended to anyone who wants to investigate the ineffective and often damaging method of managing children's behavior through rewards and punishment. The following excerpts are from *Punished by Rewards*.

Alfie Kohn on Rewards

The unsettling news is that rewards and punishments are worthless at best, and destructive at worst, for helping children develop such values and skills. What rewards and punishments do produce is temporary compliance. *They buy us obedience. If that's what we mean when we say they "work," then yes, they work wonders.*

But if we are ultimately concerned with the kind of people our children will become, there are no shortcuts. Good values have to be grown from the inside out. Praise, privileges, and punishment can change behavior (for a while), but they cannot change the person who engages in the behavior, at least not in the way we want. No behavioral manipulation ever helped a child develop a commitment to becoming a caring and responsible person. No reward for doing something we approve of ever gave a child a reason for continuing to act that way when there was no longer any reward to be gained for doing so.

Alfie Kohn on Punishment

We convince ourselves that we are not just imposing our will, but teaching the child what happens when he misbehaves, and that this will prevent future misbehavior. Moreover, we see ourselves as administering an elemental sort of justice: having broken a rule, the child must now be punished.

. . . The first rationale is fatally flawed; punishment teaches about the use of power, not about how or why to

behave properly. . . . The commitment to punishing chil-
dren typically reflects a fear that the failure to respond this
way will mean that they "got away with something."

. . . In my view, there are two fundamentally different
ways one can respond to a child who does something
wrong. One is to impose a punitive consequence. Another
is to see the situation as a "teachable moment," an oppor-
tunity to educate or to solve a problem together. The re-
sponse here is not, "You've misbehaved; now here's what
I'm going to do to you," but "Something has gone wrong;
what can we do about it?"

. . . [Constance] Kamii, drawing from [Jean] Piaget's
work, argued that punishment leads to three possible out-
comes: "calculation of risks" (which means children spend
their time figuring out whether they can get away with
something), "blind conformity" (which fails to teach re-
sponsible decision making), or "revolt." [Kamii, 1984, pp.
11, 14] . . . Piaget put this point more succinctly: "pun-
ishment . . . renders autonomy of conscience impossible."
[Piaget, 1965, p. 339].

Teaching Children Self-Control

WHEN IT IS suggested that adults should eliminate punishment, they often react by saying, "Are you kidding? Are you
suggesting I let children do whatever they want?" And the answer is "Absolutely not—children *need* discipline. That is not
the issue." What they do *not* need is punishment.

Many parents and teachers ask, "If not rewards and punishment, then what?" In response to this question I ask, "How
will children ever learn an internal locus of control (self-
control) when their only experience is an external locus of control (from parents and teachers)?"

The purpose of positive time-out—and other positive-discipline methods—is to help children learn responsibility, self-discipline, self-confidence, and self-control. Positive time-out is one of many nonpunitive ways to help children improve their behavior by empowering them to make changes.

Rewards and punishment can be replaced by respectfully involving children in the exploration of their choices. Often, positive time-out is required before this can be accomplished. Sometimes asking a child to put the problem on a class- or family-meeting agenda will serve as a cooling-off period until the next meeting. Then the whole class or family can engage in brainstorming for solutions. This teaches children that objective opinions can be very valuable. When children are upset, they cannot think rationally. Once children have taken some positive time-out to calm down and feel better, parents or

teachers can help them explore what happened, what caused it to happen, how they feel about what happened, what they learned from it, and what ideas they have to avoid the problem in the future or to solve the problem now.

Exploration Through What and How Questions

ASKING WHAT AND how questions is an extremely valuable discipline tool. The true meaning of education comes from the root word *educare,* which means "to draw forth." Too often adults try to stuff knowledge in through lectures. They tell children what happened, what caused it to happen, how they should feel about it, and what they should do about it. Then these same adults wonder why their lectures seem to go in one ear and out the other. Asking what and how questions, rather than dictating information, helps children explore through their own thinking abilities. In other words, what and how questions help draw forth children's thinking abilities.

> The true meaning of education comes from the root word *educare,* which means "to draw forth." Too often adults try to stuff knowledge in through lectures.

Since lectures and punishment are not very effective, why do adults keep using these methods? There are two main reasons: conditioning and failing to think about the long-range results. We have discussed the long-range results over and over already and will continue to do so in an attempt to get through the conditioning.

"But I Was Punished and Controlled and It Worked for Me"

MANY PARENTS AND teachers who believe in the necessity of control were raised by authoritarian, controlling parents. Their argument for continuing to use punishment and control is that it worked for them. People who use this argument are not up with the times in terms of what "works" means. It may have appeared to work, but many adults who were raised by controlling parents and teachers have the disease of perfectionism. Some are afraid that they lose self-worth if they make mistakes. Others are controlling because they have a fear of losing control. Many have not learned to focus on cooperative solutions instead of control and punishment. We could have a whole discussion about how punishment was not really as effective as many adults claim it was at teaching them to be capable, confident risk takers who value the opportunity to learn from mistakes because they were taught problem-solving skills.

Control does seem to work when children are young enough—and small enough—to be physically moved and controlled. There is, however, a time bomb built into raising children with control (and the punishment that frequently accompanies this control)—the children grow up. And what happens when children become adolescents, too large and too strong-willed to be controlled easily? Power struggles!

There are many reasons why punishment does not work on children today. One is that children no longer have models of submissiveness. Their parents are rarely submissive to each other or in the workplace. Their sports heroes are not submissive. The role models they watch on television are not submissive. In fact, many of these heroes and role models teach aggressiveness, lack of patience, lack of judgment, and lack of consideration for others and for the long-range consequences of their choices. When these children encounter punitive adults, they often become rebellious, revengeful, or sneaky; they learn to avoid getting caught.

> There are many reasons why punishment does not work on children today. One is that children no longer have models of submissiveness.

Conditioning to Conventional Wisdom Is Very Strong

BREAKING THROUGH THE conventional wisdom that children have to suffer to learn is not an easy task. Several years ago I was invited to be on the *Oprah Winfrey Show* to discuss the age-old controversy over spanking. The guests included two parents who believed in spanking and two who did not. Of course, I appreciated the parents who didn't spank and thought they were doing an excellent job. To my horror, they were labeled "permissive parents" on the television monitor. They were not at all permissive. They believed in positive discipline. These positive parents used a time-out chair (called "the happy chair") with their three-year-old. When their child misbehaved, they often asked him to sit in the happy chair until he felt better.

The father who believed in spanking made fun of this idea. He said (I will paraphrase), "Suppose both our kids go to a store and are tempted to steal something. My son will think, 'I'd better not or my parents will kill me.' Your son will think, 'If I do, my parents might make me sit in the happy chair.'" Everyone laughed because it sounded ludicrous that the threat of a happy chair would eliminate the temptation to steal.

I wanted to say to that father (but did not get the chance on the show), "Your child may not steal because he is afraid you might kill him. What will he do when you are not around to make such threats? He will not learn self-discipline and motivation when driven only by your threats."

Another time I was interviewed on a radio show in Phoenix, Arizona, where I explained the philosophy of sending kids to their rooms to cool off and feel better instead of as a punishment to make them feel bad. I suggested explaining to children that whenever they are in such a bad mood that they need time-out, they can go to their room and read a book, play with their toys, listen to music, or just rest awhile. When they feel better, they can come out and work on a solution or simply change their behavior.

I was driving down the street listening to the radio after the show and heard the host making fun of the positive time-out philosophy. "Can you imagine," he asked, "rewarding misbehavior by telling your kids to go to their room and do something to make themselves feel better?" He and many others are convinced that kids have to suffer to learn. He could not hear the part that goes beyond just feeling good to "coming out of the room when ready to work on solutions or to change behavior."

I have used two chapters (this one and Chapter 1) in an attempt to break through the conventional wisdom that punishment and punitive time-out are effective motivators. Perhaps the chart on page 50 will help. As you study this chart, notice which kind of time-out would make you feel worse and which would make you feel—and motivate you to do—better.

Eliminate Punishment and Rewards

ELIMINATING PUNISHMENT AND rewards is essential for time-out to be positive and helpful to kids. Eliminating the

The Difference Between Traditional, Negative Time-Out and Positive Time-Out

NEGATIVE TIME-OUT	POSITIVE TIME-OUT
Punitive	Nonpunitive
Discourages	Encourages
Creates distance and hostility	Creates closeness and trust
Focus is on past (pay for past)	Focus is on future (learn for future)
Focus is on blame	Focus is on solutions
Pay for deed	Learn from deed
Based on belief that children will do better if they feel worse	Based on belief that children do better when they feel better
Control (invites rebellion)	Self-control (invites cooperation)
External locus of control	Internal locus of control
Children treated as objects	Children treated as partners in the process
Invites rebellion	Invites self-discipline
Children go into survival mode	Children thrive
Reptilian brain (fight or flight)	Cortex (rational thinking)
Deals with problem at time of conflict	Allows for cooling-off time to gain perspective when thinking is irrational
Creates rebellion or unhealthy compliance when forced	Empowers when chosen (Would it help you?)
Unloving	Loving

word *punishment* from our vocabulary may be the first step in eliminating the belief that punishment is a good motivator for improved behavior.

Another step that helps us see the folly of punishment and rewards is to spend more time "getting into the child's world" to understand why they do what they do and what motivates long-term change. This is covered in the next chapter.

5

Understanding the Mistaken Goals of Behavior

A MISBEHAVING CHILD is a discouraged child (Dreikurs, 1964). Of course, this rule has exceptions, which are discussed later in this chapter. This discouragement is based on the child's belief (mistaken or not) that, "I don't belong. I'm not significant." Children aren't consciously aware of their beliefs, yet these beliefs are powerful motivators for their actions. Children who believe they don't belong and that they are not significant usually choose mistaken ways (misbehavior) to find belonging and significance. These are called mistaken goals of behavior because the results are the opposite of what a child is trying to accomplish. Instead of achieving a sense of belonging and significance, the child's misbehavior invites negative reactions from adults. When all that misbehaving children really want is to belong and feel significant, they usually get blame, shame, and pain in some form of punishment from their mistaken-goal behavior.

When all that misbehaving children really want is to belong and feel significant, they usually get blame, shame, and pain in some form of punishment from their mistaken-goal behavior.

Punitive Time-Out Discourages Children and Increases Misbehavior

WHETHER THE MISBEHAVIOR is due to discouragement, developmental readiness, or lack of skills, punitive time-out, which punishes and humiliates, only deepens the discouragement. How can anyone feel belonging and significance when banished to the isolation of punitive time-out? As I have said many times, punitive time-out may stop the behavior for the moment, but it is likely to increase discouragement and future misbehavior.

Punitive Time-Out Epitomizes Lack of Belonging

SHUNNING WAS A PUNISHMENT used by many Indian tribes and other cultures as the ultimate punishment. They were saying to the shunned, "You no longer belong to our tribe, community, or family. We will not speak to you, see you, or acknowledge you in any way. It is as though you don't exist." If perceptions of not belonging are a basis for misbehaving, how can punitive time-out improve behavior?

It is also important to understand gender issues. Some boys may feel delighted about being sent to time-out—even punitive time-out. These boys may enjoy the alone time. On the other hand, some girls may find being part of the social group to be more important, so punitive time-out may feel like shunning to them.

Positive Time-Out Encourages and Empowers Children

AS POINTED OUT in previous chapters, positive time-out can encourage and empower children. The encouragement and empowerment are increased when children helped create the positive time-out area and when they choose it because they understand that time-out can help them, not hurt them. They feel belonging and significance when they are included in the discipline process in respectful ways.

Belief Behind the Behavior

WHETHER YOU'RE AN adult or a child and whether you're conscious of it or not, there is a belief behind your behavior. Before you decide on an appropriate course of action, be it time-out or some other form of positive discipline, you will be more effective if you understand what that belief is.

It is important to remember that children are not consciously aware of the decisions they make; however, these decisions are powerful motivators for behavior. The decisions they make fall into four categories (see box on page 56).

For example, two children may decide "I am little. Others are big. The world is threatening." One child's response to this thought is "I'd better play it safe and get others to take care of me," while the other child responds "I will prove that I can take care of myself and will someday pass them all." Of course, every child makes unique decisions, but the themes about how to survive or thrive may be similar. I define *thriving* as developing skills and beliefs about being a capable, contributing,

CATEGORIES OF DECISIONS THAT CHILDREN MAKE

1. **Decisions about self:** Am I good or bad, capable or incapable, fearful or confident?

2. **Decisions about others:** Are others helpful or hurtful, nurturing or rejecting, encouraging or punitive?

3. **Decisions about the world:** Is the world safe or threatening, a joyful place or a scary place?

4. **Decisions about how to survive or thrive:** I must _____ to survive or to thrive. (When children make decisions about thriving, they are developing into capable people. When they make decisions about surviving, adults call it misbehavior.)

content member of society. *Surviving* is just another word for misbehavior based on discouraging beliefs. When children don't believe that they belong and are significant, they choose mistaken methods (misbehavior) to survive the discouragement they feel. It could be very helpful for adults to realize that behavior is based on the subconscious decisions children are always making.

Another example involves a two-year-old who feels dethroned by the birth of a new baby. The two-year-old observes all the time and attention Mom gives the new baby and *believes*, "Mom doesn't love me as much as she loves that baby." The truth doesn't matter; the child's behavior will be based on what she believes to be true. It is typical for young children who believe that they have been replaced by a new baby to act like babies. This behavior is based on the belief that "Mom will give me more time and attention if I act like the baby."

MISTAKEN GOALS OF BEHAVIOR

Undue attention	Revenge
Misguided power	Assumed inadequacy

Different children demonstrate their discouragement about their perceptions of not belonging and feeling significant in different ways. Dreikurs (1964) defined four mistaken goals of behavior (above) that children choose—usually unconsciously—when they feel they do not belong or have significance.

The goals are *mistaken goals* because a child mistakenly believes that this behavior will lead to belonging and significance. The Mistaken Goal Chart, on pages 58–59, defines the four mistaken goals of behavior and the beliefs behind each.

Different children demonstrate their discouragement about their perceptions of not belonging and feeling significant in different ways.

Understanding the Coded Message

THERE IS A coded message behind each mistaken-goal behavior. Understanding what the child is really saying through behavior will help you be more effective in dealing with that child in ways that will be encouraging, which means helping the child stop misbehaving because of changed beliefs. For example, the coded message for Undue Attention is "Notice me.

Mistaken Goal Chart

THE CHILD'S GOAL IS:	IF THE PARENT/ TEACHER FEELS:	AND TENDS TO REACT BY:	AND IF THE CHILD'S RESPONSE IS:
Undue Attention (to keep others busy or to get special services)	Annoyed Irritated Worried Guilty	Reminding Coaxing Doing things for the child he/she could do for him/ herself	Stops temporarily, but later resumes same or another disturbing behavior
Misguided Power (to be boss)	Provoked Challenged Threatened Defeated	Fighting Giving in Thinking "You can't get away with it" or "I'll make you" Wanting to be right	Intensifies behavior Defiant compliance Feels he/she has won when parent/ teacher is upset Passive power
Revenge (to get even)	Hurt Disappointed Disbelieving Disgusted	Retaliating Getting even Thinking "How could you do this to me?"	Retaliates Intensifies Escalates the same behavior or chooses another weapon
Assumed Inadequacy (to give up and be left alone)	Despair Hopeless Helpless Inadequate	Giving up Doing for Overhelping	Retreats further Passive No improvement No response

The belief behind the behavior is:	Coded Messages	Parent/teacher proactive and empowering responses include:
I count (belong) only when I'm being noticed or getting special service. I'm only important when I'm keeping you busy with me.	Notice Me; Involve Me	"I love you and . . ." (Example: "I care about you and will spend time with you later."); redirect by assigning a task so child can gain useful attention; avoid special service; plan special time; set up routines; use problem solving; encourage; use family/class meetings; touch without words; ignore; set up nonverbal signals.
I belong only when I'm boss, in control, or proving no one can boss me. You can't make me.	Let Me Help; Give Me Choices	Redirect to positive power by asking for help; offer limited choices; don't fight and give in; withdraw from conflict; be firm and kind; act, don't talk; decide what you will do; let routines be the boss; leave and calm down; develop mutual respect; set a few reasonable limits; practice follow-through; encourage; use family/class meetings.
I don't think I belong so I will hurt others as I feel hurt. I can't be liked or loved.	I'm Hurting; Validate My Feelings	Acknowledge hurt feelings; avoid feeling hurt; avoid punishment and retaliation; build trust; use reflective listening; share your feelings; make amends; show you care; act, don't talk; encourage strengths; put kids in same boat; use family/class meetings.
I can't belong because I'm not perfect, so I'll convince others not to expect anything of me; I am helpless and unable; it's no use trying because I won't do it right.	Have Faith in Me; Show Me a Small Step	Break task down into small steps; stop all criticism; encourage any positive attempt; have faith in child's abilities; focus on assets; don't pity; don't give up; set up opportunities for success; teach skills/show how, but don't do for; enjoy the child; build on his/her interests; encourage; use family/class meetings.

Involve me." Thus, a better method for helping this child would be to ignore the undue attention behavior and redirect the child by giving him a task where he can get attention by being usefully involved. (See other ideas in the last column of the Mistaken Goal Chart.)

For Misguided Power, the coded message is "Let me help. Give me choices." So, again, the best way to deal with this mistaken goal is first to admit that you can't make the child do what you want and then to let her know that you need her help. Then give her a choice of two or more ways to help. (See other ideas in the last column of the Mistaken Goal Chart.)

For Revenge, the coded message is "I'm hurting. Validate my feelings." It helps when adults can see past the revengeful behavior and validate the feelings behind it. "My guess is that you're feeling very hurt about something." Describe what you think the hurt feeling might be if you have some idea, or say, "Do you want to tell me about it?" This is often enough to disrupt the misbehavior and put the child in a mood (perhaps after a little cooling-off time) to deal with the problem, which may mean disregarding what someone else thinks, being assertive, or making amends. (See other ideas in the last column of the Mistaken Goal Chart.)

For Assumed Inadequacy, the coded message is "Have faith in me. Show me a small step." Adults need to find the smallest step the child can take. This may mean doing a step with the child until he can do it by himself. Once the child has had a small success, he will give up the idea that he is inadequate. (See other ideas in the last column of the Mistaken Goal Chart.)

Same Behavior, Different Beliefs

THE SAME BEHAVIOR, such as neglected homework, could be a result of any of the four mistaken goals. Because there is a different belief (with variations on the theme) for each mistaken goal (even though the behavior is the same), it doesn't make sense to use the same discipline method for every child.

Undue Attention

A CHILD WHO seeks belonging through undue attention could believe, "If I don't do my homework, you'll pay attention to me and I'll feel special." So, although the behavior is not doing homework and/or whining to get you to help, the coded message is "notice me, involve me." How can punitive time-out help this child feel belonging and significance, and thus remove the need to misbehave? Helping the child feel belonging and significance is very simple—redirect her into getting attention by doing something useful.

Michael would whine and coax his mom and dad to help him with his homework. They felt annoyed by this; however, they were not consistent in their responses to him. Sometimes they would tell him to stop whining and would keep badgering him to do his work. This created a painful process where they would lecture and badger, Michael would do a little and then whine some more; then his parents would lecture and badger some more, until the homework finally got done and everyone was upset and exhausted. Other times his parents would feel guilty. Maybe he wasn't getting enough attention. One of his parents would then sit down and end up doing most of the homework for him. None of this helped Michael feel capable. Receiving undue attention is actually discouraging.

When his parents learned about redirecting Michael to get attention by doing something useful, they changed their behavior, and Michael changed his. Michael's parents would say something like, "You are so creative when you set the table. As soon as you are done with your homework, come let me know what special items you need (flowers, knickknacks, construction paper, and markers for special place mats) for your

creative table tonight." If he would want to set the table first, they would ask, "What do you need to do first?"

Other parents might say, "You'll be in charge of our family meeting tonight as soon as your homework is done. I wonder how you will call us to order this time?" Another possibility is to say, "Here's a little bell. I'll be close by. You can ring the bell as soon as you have completed enough of your homework to show me and give me a report. You can ring the bell three times, so why don't you decide how much you need to do for one third of your homework to be done before you ring the bell the first time." Be creative. You know your children. How could you redirect their behavior so they will get attention in a way that is useful and that makes your children feel belonging and significance?

Misguided Power

CHILDREN WHO SEEK belonging through misguided power may believe, "I'm significant only when I decide what I'll do, or at least when I don't let you decide what I will do." Children perceive adults who demand obedience or compliance from them as trying to take away their power. Sending these children to punitive time-out is likely to backfire. They are likely to sit in time-out and think about how to defeat you so they can avoid feeling that they have "lost." (Adults who insist on winning the power struggle need to think about what position that leaves for the child—the loser.)

It is much better to help "power drunk" children learn to use their power in a contributing and helpful way. Allowing them to choose positive time-out, when they have helped design the positive time-out area, gives them a sense of power, self-control, belonging, and significance. "Would it help you to go to your special time-out area until you decide what works best for you to get your homework done?" (An adult attitude and tone of voice is of paramount importance. If your attitude conveys, in any way, that you are going to make the child go to time-out until she is ready to do what you want, you are likely to invite resistance. However, if the child perceives a true opportunity to use her power for self-control and to devise a plan that works for her, you are likely to invite useful power.)

Another possibility is to ask the child, "What is next on the 'Afternoon Routine Chart'?" (The creation of a routine chart is taught in Chapter 10.) The child then uses his power to check the chart (if he doesn't have it memorized). This serves as a reminder of how he used his power to help create the routine chart in the first place. It is usually effective to give these children a choice: "Do you want to use your old plan for getting your homework done, or do you want to write up a new one and show it to me?"

Parents who don't believe these methods will work may have created (with their children) such a strong power-struggle atmosphere that it seems difficult to change. This could be due to two things:

1. Parents haven't really decided to give up control because they don't have faith in their child to do what is best for him or her when treated respectfully.

2. If parents have decided to give up control and have faith in their child, it could be that it will take a while for the child to trust that the parents mean what they say.

If the former is true, adults should take responsibility that this attitude is a big factor in creating the power struggle. If the latter is true, adults should tell the truth about it. For example, "I have been so controlling in the past that it may be difficult for you to trust that I will treat you with respect, that I will truly involve you in finding solutions, and that I have faith in you to do what is right for you. However, I will keep treating you with respect, I will keep asking you to work with me to find solutions that work for both of us, and I will keep having faith in you. I hope you can trust me soon."

Revenge

A CHILD SEEKING revenge has given up on belonging, but believes, "At least I can get even with you for how much you (or someone else, or something) have hurt me, and I know it upsets you if I don't do my homework."

The sad thing about revenge is that children usually choose a behavior that hurts them at least as much as it hurts the adults with whom they are trying to get even. Punitive time-out only increases the revenge cycle. The child is likely to sit in punitive time-out to feed feelings of revenge and to think of ways to get even.

The first step to encourage a child who is hurt is to validate her feelings through reflective listening. This is not easy to do if you have covered up your own hurt feelings to engage in the revenge cycle. (Anger is often a cover-up for hurt feelings.) However, when you understand the "code" of the child's behavior, you may be able to look at your own hurt feelings, which will give you a clue to what she feels hurt about. This is not the time to tell her about your hurt feelings. Children listen to you only after they feel listened to. Later you can share your feelings.

By validating her feelings, you help her regain a sense of belonging, which will put her in a better mood to listen to you, to give or accept an apology, or to make amends for any damage she might have done. Adults can model making amends by being the first to apologize, even if they didn't mean to be hurtful. Children are very forgiving when they hear a sincere apology and will often follow with an apology of their own.

When a child experiences validations for feelings (and feels understood), this is often enough to help her give up belief that she doesn't belong, and thus her desire for revenge. Most adults underestimate the power of validation for the child who is seeking revenge. It may take some positive time-out to allow the message to sink in and for wounds to heal. It is very important to give this child a choice about going to time-out alone, with you, or with another student. Let her know, "As soon as you feel better, we can talk more about this and see what else we might need to do."

Assumed Inadequacy

A CHILD WHOSE goal is assumed inadequacy (giving up) believes, "I can't be significant no matter what I do. I give up. Leave me alone." I can't imagine anyone sending this child to any kind of time-out—negative or positive.

It takes a lot of understanding and patience to be effective with this child. It is very easy to fall into the trap of believing he can't be helped. Children seeking undue attention and children feeling assumed inadequacy might say, "I can't." However, with the child who is seeking undue attention, you know and she knows that she really can; thus you might feel annoyed. With the child feeling assumed inadequacy, you know he doesn't believe he can, and you may feel despair and

inadequacy about how to motivate him to change this belief. There is usually a temptation to do things for the child, which will only deepen his belief that he is inadequate. The most effective way to encourage this child is to break things down into smaller steps. Keep making it simpler until he can't believe he can't. You might show him a very small step and then be sure he does it on his own to be sure he can feel successful.

Long-Range Results of Ignoring the Belief Behind the Behavior

TOO OFTEN WE deal with behavior alone and fail to recognize the belief behind the behavior. This is similar to putting out fires while ignoring the arsonist who sets them. Yes, parents and teachers must put out the fires; but the fires will stop only when adults deal with the arsonist. They need to deal with misbehavior and make every effort to understand the belief behind it.

Putting children in punitive time-out without considering the belief behind their behavior is likely to cause them to develop more negative beliefs that will lead to more misbehavior. A recurring theme of this book is the importance of considering the long-range effects of what we do. One of the most effective ways to do this is to get into the child's world. Goal disclosure is an excellent way to get into the children's world, to diagnose children's mistaken goal, and to help them understand their behavior.

Goal Disclosure

AS HAS BEEN stated earlier, children are not aware of their beliefs and mistaken goals. Goal disclosure helps them become aware of what they are doing and why; it can also help them find more effective ways to achieve their goals of belonging and feeling significant. To be effective with goal disclosure, you must show a friendly attitude and genuinely want to know what the child believes.

Sometimes, just the process of goal disclosure can be encouraging to a child. Take Shaun for example. Shaun was in Mrs. Williams's third-grade class. Mrs. Williams noticed that Shaun went to the positive time-out area several times a day. Mrs. Williams checked into her feelings about Shaun and realized that she felt inadequate in her attempts to motivate him to learn. This was her first clue that Shaun was in Assumed Inadequacy. Mrs. Williams decided to do goal disclosure with Shaun to check out her hunch, to help him be aware of his mistaken goal, and to enhance their relationship.

When Shaun came in after school, Mrs. Williams set up a friendly atmosphere by first asking him if he had noticed the fascinating cloud formations. Each tried to pick out patterns. Mrs. Williams showed Shaun a rabbit; Shaun pointed out a kite.

Then Mrs. Williams said, "Shaun, I have noticed that you have been going into time-out a lot. Do you know why you are using time out so much?"

Shaun said, "I need a cooling-off time to help me feel better." (Kids usually say, "I don't know," but not always.)

THE PROCESS OF GOAL DISCLOSURE

1. Ask the child why he or she is doing a certain behavior, even though you know the answer will most likely be, "I don't know."

2. Ask permission to guess why. Most children will give you permission if you have shown them you are friendly and really care about how they feel. You probably suspect the goal before using goal disclosure; you simply need verification from the child (parents and teachers can—occasionally—be wrong). Let children know they can tell you if you are wrong, which usually piques their interest.

3. Ask, "Could it be _____?" regarding each mistaken goal, as demonstrated by Mrs. Williams.

Mrs. Williams said, "That may be the reason, but I have another idea. I don't know for sure, but would it be okay with you if I make a couple of guesses?" (It's important to say you don't know, but want to guess, because that's the truth.) "You can let me know if I'm right or wrong."

Shaun looked uncertain, but said, "I guess so."

Mrs. Williams asked, "Could it be that using time-out is a good way to get my attention and keep me busy with you?"

With a straight face, Shaun said, "No." (It is important to look for a recognition reflex with the answer. If Shaun had said no with a grin on his face, he might actually have been saying yes. When you get a recognition reflex, you acknowledge it by saying something like, "Shaun, your voice says no, but your smile is telling me that could be the reason.")

Mrs. Williams said, "May I guess again?"

Shaun was intrigued; he agreed.

"Could it be that using time-out is a good way to show that you are in charge and can do what you want?"

Again Shaun said no with no recognition reflex.

Mrs. Williams asked, "Could it be that the reason you use time-out a lot is that you feel hurt and want to hurt others by withdrawing from us?"

Shaun said, "No."

Mrs. Williams said, "May I guess one more time?"

Shaun agreed again.

"Could it be that you feel you can't do your work and just want to give up?"

Shaun got a tear in his eye and whispered, "I can't."

Mrs. Williams said, "Shaun, I'm so glad to know that's what you think. I can help you with that. Let's work on a plan together, because I know you can. You just need a little more help." It can be very encouraging for a child feeling Assumed Inadequacy to hear that his teacher or parent believes in him and will help him (but not do it for him).

If Mrs. Williams had received an affirmative or a "giveaway grin" to any of the goal disclosure questions, she would not need to proceed with the other questions. Earlier it was said that children are not conscious of their decisions. Goal disclosure can bring the decision to the surface and help the child feel understood. It can also give the parent or teacher an understanding of how to help.

No matter what the goal, you can work on a plan with the child to solve the problem. For attention, you can work out useful ways to get attention, and you can make a point of giving attention periodically for no reason at all except to show you care. For power, you can find constructive ways for the child to be powerful. For revenge, you can talk about hurt feelings. Acknowledging the hurt is often enough to straighten out the cause of the revenge.

Since Shaun's goal was giving up, Mrs. Williams spent extra time tutoring him until she was sure he understood the work and could achieve success. "It didn't really take much extra time," she explained later. "I would just be encouraging for an extra minute or two, which can seem like an eternity to a child who wants to give up. At first Shaun insisted he couldn't do it. Then it seemed as if he did it just to get me off his back. I remember the surprised, pleased look on his face the first time he *didn't* give up and successfully completed his work."

A child with the mistaken goal of giving up does not enjoy extra attention the way a child with the mistaken goal of attention does. This child may try to "disappear," which is often one clue to help you figure out the mistaken goal.

Part of the plan Mrs. Williams worked out with Shaun was for him to choose a classmate to work with until he felt confident to work on his own. Shaun also agreed to tutor a first grader who needed help at a level where Shaun felt confidence. Shaun's sense of belonging and significance improved when he learned both to give and to receive help.

Goal disclosure can help children become consciously aware of their mistaken goals. Awareness increases responsibility, choice, and possible change. The Mistaken Goal Chart

offers several suggestions, other than time-out, for behavior based on any of the four mistaken goals.

Teaching the Mistaken Goals of Behavior to Children

MANY PARENTS AND teachers talk openly with their children and students about the mistaken goals of behavior. They let the children know there is a useful side to attention and power, as well as a useless side. Children on the useless side of attention and power usually respond to a request for help so they can gain attention or power through contribution.

One activity that gets children involved and increases their awareness is brainstorming with them ways that are not useful and ways that are useful for gaining attention. To do this, use a flip chart or large sheet of paper with *Attention* as the main heading and with two columns: one for *Useless* and one for *Useful.* Write (or have a child write) every useful and useless idea the children think of. Then do the same for power, with a column for *Useful* and one for *Useless.* These sheets of paper can be hung on a wall to serve as reminders.

Children can also brainstorm ways to help a person who feels hurt and ways to encourage a person who feels inadequate. Most children feel inspired to help others when they learn to understand the discouragement behind misbehavior and when they are given the opportunity to help.

Children Can Remind Parents

MARGARET AND HER nine-year-old son Rod were having an argument. Rod's father and Margaret had divorced recently, and mother and son were both still adjusting to their new lifestyle.

"Time to clean up your room and get ready for bed, Rod. School tomorrow," Margaret announced.

"But Mom, I'm still working on this model," Rod answered. "Can I stay up just a little while longer?"

Margaret had had a long day; work had been stressful, the bills seemed to be piling up faster than she could pay them, and the sink was full of dishes. She answered with more irritation in her voice than she intended, "No, young man. I said now, and I mean *now*."

Rod's frustration equaled his mother's, and his reply was meant to sting. "You're *always* grumpy these days," he shot back. "I'd rather go live with my dad. He never tells me what to do, and we have fun together. I know why he divorced you; who'd want to live with a grump?"

The door closed with a loud thump, and Margaret could hear Rod angrily putting away his things. She resisted the impulse to burst through the door and respond to her son's painful, and unfair, accusations. She knew that she needed time to cool off and that behind his closed door Rod was doing some thinking of his own.

After a short while, Margaret heard the door open, and a quiet voice said, "Mom, can we work this out?"

Margaret and her son sat down and talked about what had happened and why, about revenge and why we sometimes strike back to hurt even people we love. They talked about their situation and how they both needed time to adjust. Margaret explained that the anger in her voice had more to do with work and stress than it did with Rod, while Rod apologized for having said things he knew would cause his mother pain. Both agreed that they needed time to cool off and to think before they spoke.

Margaret had the courage to live the principle that mistakes truly are opportunities to learn and that help from each other is something to welcome rather than avoid. This example teaches that there are times when we might be too upset to welcome help. At those times it helps to take time-out until we have calmed down and feel better. Margaret and her son have learned that time-out is not the final solution; rather it is a time to think, to feel better, and to get ready for productive solutions.

6

Will Children Ever Just Mind?

A Case for Encouragement

HAVE YOU EVER wondered if there is a time or an age at which children will just do as they are told—the first time—without you having to nag? Or have you ever wondered if there is a time or an age at which children will just do what they know they are supposed to do—again, without lectures or nagging? If so, you are not alone.

Doesn't it make sense to expect that children will just say, "Sure, Mom and Dad, I'll be happy to do what you ask right now. And I can't tell you how much I appreciate all you do for me." Welcome to fairyland.

Unfortunately, children often don't do what they are told to do by parents and teachers, at least not all of the time. I don't even know of many adults who do what they are supposed to do—all of the time. Many of us eat things we know we aren't supposed to eat; are judgmental of others, even when we know we aren't supposed to be; may be late, tell little white lies, or procrastinate, even when we know we aren't supposed to. And we often resist requests from spouses and equals—just because. Just because what?

Why Children and Adults Resist Requests

UNDERSTANDING WHY ADULTS often resist a simple request might give us some clues as to why children resist. There are other factors for children, which will be addressed later, but, first, let's see what we have in common: When a spouse or equal asks you to do something, do you think or feel any of the following?

1. If I do what is requested, I'm letting this person control me.

2. Why should I do what this person requests when it is important to him or her, but doesn't matter to me? Why doesn't he or she lighten up and get a life?

3. Can't he or she see I have other things to do? Doesn't he or she think what I'm doing is important—and yes, that means even when I'm resting?

4. Why would I want to do anything when I'm asked in that tone of voice?

5. Who does he or she think I am—a slave?

Most of these issues have to do with respect. Adults and children often feel a lack of respect when asked to do something. Later we discuss how to increase chances for cooperation by making requests respectfully (and especially by getting children respectfully involved). But first we need to discuss the other reasons why children may not cooperate and why they don't always do what they know they are supposed to do, even if the request is respectful.

Why Children Resist

1. Things they are supposed to do aren't high on their priority list—if they're on the list at all. Those things are on the *adult's* priority list. Children don't really care if the house is clean, if the lawn is mowed, if they are dressed on time, if they come to dinner on time, and so on. They often don't see the relevancy of their homework. Does this mean they shouldn't do these things? No. For now, we are just discussing why they don't.

2. Children are individuating, which means they are in a continual process of finding out who they are—separate from the adults in their lives. How can they individuate without a little test of wills and boundaries; without trying the opposite of what their parents and teachers ask? The most profound spurt of individuation takes place when children reach adolescence, but smaller spurts occur throughout the growing years. Obedient robots will never become healthy, individuated adults.

3. And, of course, there is mistaken goal behavior when children don't believe they belong. Some children don't do what they are supposed to do as a way of getting undue attention, of showing misguided power, to get revenge for a real or perceived injustice, or because of assumed inadequacy.

Parents are usually part of the problem when mistaken goal behavior is taking place, but it is usually children who get the blame. For example, I have never seen a power-drunk child without a power-drunk adult really close by.

A Parent's and Teacher's Job Is Never Done

THE REASONS FOR misbehavior are why the job of parents and teachers is never done. They are also why we need to keep using positive time-out and other positive-discipline methods over and over. These positive methods are the most effective way to continue encouraging cooperation, even though that cooperation doesn't last forever. Dishes don't stay clean, floors don't stay mopped, and children don't always do what they know they are supposed to do. We can rage about this, or we can accept it and find joyful ways to discipline.

Attitude and Skills

AN ATTITUDE OF understanding and acceptance will bring peace. Parenting and teaching skills that increase cooperation will help you and your children and/or students enjoy positive long-range results, such as important life skills for success (becoming happy, contributing members of society) and perceptions of courage, confidence, and competence (developing healthy self-esteem). The foundation for all of these discipline skills (as discussed many times in this book) is kindness and firmness at the same time: kindness to show respect for the child, and firmness to show respect for what needs to be done. This is the basis for encouragement, and encouragement is the key.

Encouragement

CHAPTER 5 EXPLAINED that a misbehaving child is a discouraged child, and this discouragement is based on the child's belief (mistaken or not) that, "I don't belong. I'm not significant." Because misbehavior is due to discouragement, does punitive time-out ever make sense? Of course not. Punitive time-out only further discourages children, and thus increases the likelihood of increased misbehavior. And how can it possibly make sense to put small children in time-out when their behavior is developmentally appropriate (even if we don't like it) or due to lack of skills? For example, it is developmentally appropriate for a toddler to cry when frustrated because she has not yet developed the words or skills to deal with her frustration. It is developmentally appropriate for a toddler to want to explore the wall sockets, even though she has been told many times not to do so. This is why supervision, distraction, and redirection are better discipline tools for this age.

Because misbehavior can be motivated by discouragement, it follows that the best way to eliminate misbehavior is to encourage children: help them feel that they belong and are significant. Positive time out can help children feel encouraged—a concept that can be very difficult for many adults to grasp. Adults often don't think it feels right to encourage a child who has misbehaved. In their minds, encouragement would be the same as rewarding misbehavior or being permissive. (See Chapter 4 for a discussion of why this is not so.)

Age-Appropriate Strategies

ADULTS WHO DON'T understand that children do better when they feel better may be saying, "Oh terrific; I know some teenagers who would take this 'feel good' idea and run with it!" One high school teacher expressed concern about allowing high school students to create a time-out area that would make them feel good. He could just see the wild posters, hear the loud music, and smell the cigarette smoke. And he was sure that most teens would go out of their way to have time-out in such a cool place.

He is right. The developmental stage of adolescence (individuation and testing personal power) is one reason a really "cool" time-out area may not be a good idea. However, some high school teachers have found positive time-out to be successful with their students, as mentioned in Chapter 2. The key to success for these teachers was that they provided a learning environment where students wanted to be, and the students were involved in planning the time-out. The class discussed the issue of students taking advantage of time-out and decided that those who abused the opportunity would lose it.

Using or Losing Influence

WHEN ADULTS HELP children feel better (encouraged), they create closeness and trust. When children can trust the adults in their lives, they have less incentive to misbehave and more opportunity to learn the positive, long-term skills of responsibility and self-discipline. When adults and children have a foundation of closeness and trust, adults have influence to help children develop the skills they need to control their behavior.

> When children can trust the adults in their lives, they have less incentive to misbehave and more opportunity to learn the positive, long-term skills of responsibility and self-discipline.

When adults insist on remaining in full control, when they resort to punishment and humiliation, they create resistance and hostility in their children, and they lose the opportunity for trust and positive influence.

Positive Time-Out Sets the Stage for Learning

POSITIVE TIME-OUT (encouragement) is only the first step. Once children feel better, they are ready to do better. Once

they feel encouraged, they are ready to explore the consequences of their choices, or to work on a solution, or to make amends if appropriate.

It is not helpful to try communicating when you or your child is upset. (Remember, this is when the primitive brain takes over, and you and your child or student are not capable of rational communication and/or learning.) Positive time-out allows time for the rational brain to take over again so respectful communication and problem solving can take place.

John Taylor's Thermometer

IN HIS BOOK *Person to Person*, John Taylor (1984) describes a role-play activity that helps adults understand a child's perceptions and experience the difference between closeness and trust and distance and hostility.

One adult volunteer plays a child and another is the adult. The two start out facing each other about four feet apart. The "child" is told: "Whenever the 'adult' says something that makes you feel encouraged, move toward him. Whenever the 'adult' says something that makes you feel discouraged, move further away. Do not respond verbally." The "adult" is then instructed, "Start out by making punitive statements intended to make the 'child' feel guilty or bad. Then change your tactics and make positive statements to help the 'child' feel understood and encouraged."

Here is one example of what happened when two people tried this activity:

> *Adult:* I heard you were misbehaving on the play-ground again! When are you going to learn to be more respectful? (Child moves away.)
>
> *Adult:* Well, don't you have anything to say for your-self? (Child moves further away.)
>
> *Adult:* Well, you can just sit on the time-out bench for a week and see if that will teach you! (Child moves fur-ther away.)
>
> *Adult (using a friendly voice):* I heard there was a prob-lem on the playground, and I would really like to hear your side of the story. (Child moves closer.)
>
> *Adult:* I can understand why you feel upset; sometimes I feel the same way. (Child moves closer.)
>
> *Adult:* Would you be willing to do something to help you feel better until you can work on a solution? (Child moves closer.)
>
> *Adult:* Why don't you decide how much time you need on the feel-good bench, and we'll give the other child the same opportunity. (Child moves closer.)

When the adult approached the child in an accusing man-ner, the child backed away. In other words, the adult lost influ-ence. When the adult approached the child in a friendly, understanding manner, the adult then had influence to help the child consider solutions (after choosing some positive time-out).

Things Often Get Worse Before They Get Better

WE LIVE IN a "fast-food" society; sometimes we expect that when we make changes, we will see instant results. We have been programmed to think of time-out as a punishment for misbehavior rather than as an encouraging way to solve a problem, and it can take time for old attitudes to change—both for us and for our children.

It takes time for both adults and children to absorb the idea that time-out can be a positive, encouraging experience rather than just another form of punishment. It may be helpful to remind children occasionally that we don't want them to feel bad; we want them to feel better.

> Change won't happen overnight; but anything that not only helps a child improve behavior but also encourages and builds a sense of belonging, significance, self-control, and self-discipline is worth the time and effort it takes.

It is well worth the effort and time it takes (usually three to six weeks) for children and adults to get used to positive time-out. Change won't happen overnight; but anything that not only helps a child improve behavior but also encourages and builds a sense of belonging, significance, self-control, and self-discipline is worth the time and effort it takes.

Perhaps the most effective parenting tool is a preventive one: encouraging children, noticing their good behavior and contributions to the family and classroom, getting them involved in family and class meetings, and empowering them to solve their own problems. When children feel encouraged, the need for positive time-out—or any other positive-discipline method— can be reduced because the need to misbehave is reduced. When nothing else seems to work, find ways to encourage your children.

7

Logical Consequences

L OGICAL CONSEQUENCES ARE often as misused as time-out. As we have seen, children develop an important life skill when they learn to take time to calm down until they feel better before taking further action. The process of learning to understand the logical consequences of their choices and actions can also provide important life skills.

The misuse of logical consequences occurs when parents and teachers impose a punishment in the name of logical consequences instead of helping children understand and evaluate the consequences of their choices. After children have taken positive time-out to feel better, they may be open to exploring the consequences of their choices. Notice the word *exploring*. Children aren't exploring (evaluating) for themselves when adults are busy lecturing and punishing.

The misuse of logical consequences occurs when parents and teachers impose a punishment in the name of logical consequences instead of helping children understand and evaluate the consequences of their choices.

Exploring the Logical Consequences of Choices

EIGHT-YEAR-OLD JAKE didn't do his homework. His father confiscated his bicycle and told him he was grounded (punitive time-out) until he got it done. Dad thought this was a logical consequence for not doing homework. Jake was so angry that he sat in his room and thought about how he would refuse to do his homework or do just enough to get by to get even with his father. He certainly wouldn't do his best.

Sixteen-year-old Emma didn't do her homework, so her father asked Emma for an appointment to talk with her and asked, "Which would work best for you, 6:30 or 7:00 this evening?" (Giving Emma a choice allows her some power, which usually invites cooperation instead of defensiveness. Waiting even a short time before a discussion allows both adults and children some time-out for calmness instead of the kind of attack and defensiveness that often happens when a discussion occurs out of anger.) Emma thought she knew what was coming and chose 6:30 to get it over with.

At 6:30, Emma was surprised when her father started by asking, "I wonder if you love yourself as much as I love you?"

Emma laughed and said, "What are you talking about, Dad?"

Dad said, "Well, I just wanted to let you know how much I love you. Because of that, I have your best interests at heart. I just wondered if you love yourself as much and if you think about your best interests?"

Emma was very suspicious, "Is this your way of conning me into doing my homework.?"

Dad replied, "Why would I try to con you into doing your homework if you don't think that would be good for you? We both know I can't make you do anything you don't want to do. However, I am willing to help you explore what is good for you, and I'm willing to help you create a plan that works for you to accomplish what is best for you."

Emma said, "Okay, Dad. I'll do my homework." (When Dad invited Emma to discuss the problem instead of using lectures and punishment, which she would resist, resent, and rebel against, Emma quickly figured out that doing her homework would be in her best interest.)

However, this wasn't enough to satisfy Dad, who replied, "Honey, it doesn't work for me to have to remind you all the time. That seems to create a conflict between us. I don't want to spend our time that way. You wouldn't agree to do your homework if you didn't know that is in your best interest. How about taking it a step further. You might find it helpful to create a regular evening routine that includes the best time for you to do your homework—one that would work for you and that would take me out of the loop. You can show me what you come up with tomorrow night. I have faith in you to know what kind of plan would work best for you."

Emma agreed. The next night she showed her dad her plan (shown on the following page).

Dad said, "Looks like a good plan. Now this routine can be the boss instead of me. I think you will find this kind of organization very useful throughout your life."

Why Children Don't Cooperate

MANY PARENTS DON'T believe their children would be as cooperative as Emma was. If these parents have established a pattern of power struggles instead of guiding their children to use their own power in useful ways, then they are right—the children probably won't cooperate. What parents usually mean by *cooperate* is, "Do what I tell you to do." This definition does not invite cooperation; it invites rebellion.

> When children don't cooperate, perhaps parents and teachers have not created an environment where children are truly involved in creating plans and guidelines and brainstorming solutions. Many children have more practice in protecting their "sense of self" through resistance and rebellion instead of through self-control and cooperation.

Emma was used to having her parents turn the responsibility for her actions over to her. They had spent many hours in regular family meetings brainstorming for solutions to problems. Emma had been involved in creating routines (bedtime, morning, mealtime) since she was two years old. Although Emma's parents established this process early on in life, it is never too late to start. It is, however, helpful to know why there might be some resistance if you start late.

Exploring Logical Consequences Through What and How Questions

HELPING CHILDREN UNDERSTAND the consequences of their choices is a powerful life lesson. Sometimes it takes a series of what and how questions to help children use their own thinking ability to explore consequences. At other times, one question might be enough. However, asking what and how questions is not effective if it is used to get children to recite a script you have in mind. The point is to help them explore for themselves the consequences of their choices.

Emma's parents had often helped her explore the consequences of her choices by asking her what happened, how she felt about what happened, what she had learned, how she could use what she had learned in the future, and what ideas she had for solving the problem now. They did not ask these questions if either they or Emma were upset because they knew that the time of conflict (when people have lost perspective and are thinking irrationally) is not the best time to focus on learning and on solutions. They often used positive time-out to wait until everyone could be in a more objective mood. Sometimes they would go to their separate special time-out areas; other times they would go to time-out together; on occasion they decided to put the problem on the family-meeting agenda. Waiting for the next meeting served as a cooling-off period.

When four-year-old Riley didn't want to set the table, his mother stooped down to eye level with him and asked, "Then what will we eat on?" Riley thought about that and then said, "Oh all right." This very simple question invited Riley to think things through and to choose cooperation. Another child (or even an older Riley) might not respond the same. That is why parents need many positive-discipline tools.

When parents and teachers use logical consequences to disguise punishment, they invite children to resist, rebel, or retreat into sneakiness or low self-esteem instead of to explore. Maintaining dignity and respect is essential for logical consequences to be used effectively.

Dignity and Respect

ALL HUMAN BEINGS (and children *are* human beings) have the right to be treated with dignity and respect, even when they need to experience the consequences of their choices. Most of us will admit that our mistakes and wrong choices are often what teach us the greatest lessons. The concept of logical consequences as a form of discipline, rather than punishment, enables children to learn from their mistakes in a protected, encouraging environment.

> All human beings (and children *are* human beings) have the right to be treated with dignity and respect, even when they need to experience the consequences of their choices.

It is time to stop misusing logical consequences. When dignity and respect are lacking, logical consequences are just another form of punishment, which often includes humiliating lectures and put-downs. Logical consequences require enforcement with dignity and respect. Positive time-out can be a logical consequence when it is used under these conditions and when used with the philosophy of the Three Rs of Logical Consequences:

THE THREE Rs OF LOGICAL CONSEQUENCES

The Three Rs of Logical Consequences will help parents and teachers use logical consequences in an appropriate and positive manner.

1. **Related.** A consequence must be logically and obviously related to the behavior.

2. **Respectful.** The consequence must be enforced respectfully, without anger, force, or humiliation.

3. **Reasonable.** The consequence must seem reasonable to the child and to the adult.

Logical consequences are turned into punishment when any one of the Three Rs is not followed. Time-out is not related, respectful, or reasonable when it is used as a punishment.

Related

TIME-OUT IS RELATED only when children understand how negative feelings affect behavior. They must know that positive time-out can allow a cooling-off period to help them feel better so they can behave better. Time-out is not related when a child perceives that he or she has been "sentenced" to time-out as an arbitrary punishment for misbehavior.

Respectful

TIME-OUT IS RESPECTFUL only when children know the purpose is to help, not punish. It is respectful when the feeling behind time-out is one of dignity and respect. Maintaining dignity and respect at all times can be difficult; but it is essential and can be accomplished only when the adult involved has a tone of voice and attitude that conveys his belief that time-out is an opportunity to feel better and work toward solving a problem. Time-out is respectful when children choose it because they know it will help them. Time-out is not respectful when parents or teachers add lectures or any kind of blame, shame, or pain.

Reasonable

TIME-OUT IS REASONABLE only when it serves a reasonable purpose—to help children (and/or adults) calm down until they can think and behave rationally. Another important factor to ensure that time-out is reasonable is to help children see the value for themselves. Children will see the value of time-out when they are involved in advanced planning—for example, helping to design the time-out area (as discussed in Chapter 2).

Kind and Firm at the Same Time

STRANGE AS IT seems, when suggesting consequences, we can be kind and firm at the same time rather than humiliating and firm or angry and firm. An angry, humiliating parent or teacher would say, "You're in time-out for half an hour! Write fifty sentences about your bad behavior." A kind and firm parent or teacher says, "I can see you are too upset to behave respectfully. Some positive time-out may help you feel better.

You can decide when you're ready to work this out." Kindness invites cooperation. Punishment invites resentment and rebellion. Too often adults don't think about the long-range results of what they do and say.

Remember the Purpose of Logical Consequences

PARENTS AND TEACHERS use logical consequences in the hope that understanding the consequences will help children change their behavior and do better. This purpose is not achieved when adults misuse time-out in a punitive way and try to call it a logical consequence. Time-out and logical consequences become punitive when the focus is on the past instead of the future. In other words, when time-out is used to make kids pay for what they have done instead of to help them feel better so they will do better, it is not being used effectively. Adults can achieve their goal of helping children understand the consequences of their choices and behavior when they invite children to explore the consequences for themselves.

Another Misuse of Logical Consequences

TURNING LOGICAL CONSEQUENCES into punishment is only one danger. Another lies in thinking that logical consequences should be applied to every misbehavior (or believing that time-out is a logical consequence for every misbehavior). If you find that you are doing this, take a look at the Mistaken Goal Chart in Chapter 5. You will notice a number of possible responses to mistaken-goal behavior. Other suggestions for avoiding the misuse of logical consequences are also explained in detail throughout this book and in other *Positive Discipline* books.

A Rose (Logical Consequence) Smells Sweeter (Is More Effective) by Some Other Name

MANY ADULTS HAVE found that they use logical consequences correctly when they use a different name. As was
pointed out earlier in this chapter, logical consequences are
most effective when children learn from their choices (even
when they are mistakes) through exploration. There are times,
however, when adults can impose logical consequences. The
true intent, which is the avoidance of punishment, is apparent
when these consequences are identified by another name—a
name that conveys what the adult will do.

FIVE LOGICAL CONSEQUENCES BY ANOTHER NAME

1. Decide what you will do.

2. Follow through with kind and firm action.

3. Shut your mouth and act.

4. If you say it, mean it, and if you mean it, say it only
   once.

5. Less is more.

Decide What You Will Do

INSTEAD OF DECIDING what you will try to make a child
do, decide what you will do yourself. Deciding what you will
do is also an excellent way for you to take some positive time-
out instead of reacting and engaging in a power struggle. For
example, a teacher might refuse to teach while children are
being disruptive. Many teachers find that taking time-out for

kind and firm silence often gets children's attention much more effectively than yelling or lectures. When your action is based on kindness and firmness at the same time, it can be a powerful consequence for a child to encounter. Deciding what you will do is an excellent way for you to take some positive time-out instead of reacting and engaging in a power struggle.

> Deciding what you will do is an excellent way for you to take some positive time-out instead of reacting and engaging in a power struggle.

For example, when a child is having a tantrum in a store, kindly and firmly take his hand and leave the store. Go sit in the car and quietly read a book. (What a great positive time-out for you.) Remember that lectures invite resistance and arguments. If you say anything at all it could be, "We'll return to the store as soon as you are ready." Young children seem to catch on quicker from kind and firm action than they do from words. Sitting in the car can also give your child positive time-out to have his tantrum away from the public eye until he is ready to be respectful in public again. (In this case the time-out

is positive, even if the child didn't choose it, because you respectfully allow him to feel what he feels without adding lectures or punishment—and it is respectful to others because they don't have to listen to it.)

As another example, when children are whining, you can leave the room. (Again, you are taking time-out instead of reacting.) In other circumstances, you can say, "I'll read a story as soon as you are all ready for bed." "I'll cook only in a clean kitchen." "I will listen when you are ready to use words." "I will drive only when seat belts are buckled."

Follow Through with Kind and Firm Action

FOLLOWING THROUGH WITH kind and firm action is a part of deciding what you will do. There it is again: kind and firm. It is neither kind nor firm to sit in a chair and yell at a child to stop doing something. When all you do is yell, with no action, children often don't believe what you say. It's not until you get up and act—usually out of increased anger—that children respond, not because they are listening but because they are scared. Why not avoid the yelling and the anger and begin with what works? Follow through with kind and firm action.

Dad was sitting in his chair reading the paper. He told his two sons Ron and Jack to pick up their toys and get ready for bed. Both boys ignored him and kept playing with their toys. In about five minutes Dad raised his voice, "I told you to pick up those toys and get to bed." The boys said, "Okay," but kept playing with their toys. Finally Dad got out of his chair, gave them swats on their behinds while yelling, "Why can't you boys ever do what you are told? I'm sick and tired of this. You can just go to bed without a story, and I'm throwing these toys in the garbage." Dad used ineffective parenting skills and then punished the boys when these skills didn't work. The boys were crying and Dad was angry—not a pleasant way to end the day.

A similar scene occurred at a neighbor's house. Kenny and Gibson were playing with their toys when it was time to go to bed. Dad got out of his chair, sat on the floor with the boys, and said, "Who can tell me what time it is?" The boys didn't feel like ignoring their dad because he had come so close to them, was addressing them respectfully, and was inviting them to participate. One of the boys looked at his watch and said, "7:30." Dad asked, "And what did we decide happens at 7:30 when we created our bedtime routine chart?" The boys chimed in together. "Time to pick up our toys," as they started the task. And they were looking forward to the next item on their routine chart—a playful wrestling match with their dad for five minutes before their showers.

Even when children have made agreements in advance, and even when they have helped create routine charts, kind

Even when children have made agreements in advance, and even when they have helped create routine charts, kind and firm follow-through is the best way for parents to invite cooperation.

and firm follow-through is the best way for parents to invite cooperation. As I have said before, yelling and punishment only invite resistance.

Two-and-a-half-year-old Melanie kept hitting her one-year-old brother, Scotty. Before taking a parenting class, her mother kept threatening to spank her and put her in time-out. Melanie's mom had to laugh when the parenting leader showed a cartoon of a father spanking a child while saying, "I'll teach you not to hit other people." Then she felt like crying when she realized what she had been doing to Melanie. However, the leader offered hope through her suggestions, which Mom decided to try.

The very next night Melanie gave her mom the opportunity to practice what she had learned. Melanie bopped Scotty in the back and knocked him down for no apparent reason. Mom scooped Melanie up in her arms and gave her a hug. Scotty was still crying, but Mom believed she was doing something that could prevent a lot of future pain for Scotty. Mom whispered in Melanie's ear, "What do you think we could do to make Scotty feel better?" Melanie innocently replied, "I don't know." Mom said, "Do you think he would like a hug?" Melanie agreed. Mom said, "Do you want to give him a hug by yourself, or should we do it together?" Melanie said, "Together." So Mom scooped Scotty up on her other knee and the three of them cuddled together. Mom avoided lectures and scoldings. She had faith that modeling loving behavior would have a more powerful effect for the long-range.

The next day, Melanie was hugging Scotty so hard that he cried. Again, Mom picked up Melanie and held her softly while saying, "Shall we let Scotty join us for soft and gentle hugs?" Melanie agreed, and Mom showed her how to be very soft and gentle while hugging. Both Mom and Dad continued modeling loving behavior every time Melanie hurt Scotty. Within a few weeks, they noticed she had stopped hurting him.

As these example show, kind and firm action is much more effective than yelling and punishing.

Shut Your Mouth and Act

SHUTTING YOUR MOUTH and acting is also part of deciding what you will do and of follow-through. Many parents and teachers have a difficult time resisting lectures, scoldings, and punishment. It seems to them that they are letting a child get away with something if they don't do something to stop the behavior. Adults are also afraid that treating a child in a loving way after he or she has done something mean will reinforce the mean behavior. These fears are based on shortsighted thinking. As I have said before, punishment stops the behavior for the

Children learn what they live (what is modeled for them). Loving action is the best model you can give your children, sometimes with your mouth shut.

moment. However, what has been modeled? What is a child learning for the future?

Most children tune out lectures and scoldings; the only one listening is the parent. Punishment invites resistance, revenge, and rebellion in the long range. Although follow-through with kind and firm action may not give immediate, positive results, neither does punishment—even though parents have that illusion. Children learn what they live (what is modeled for them). Loving action is the best model you can give your children, sometimes with your mouth shut.

When you are at the park and it is time to go and your children have not responded to a kind and firm request to get in the car, shut your mouth, take them by the hand, and gently lead them to the car. If they are having a temper tantrum in the grocery store, shut your mouth and kindly and firmly take them to the car. Do not say a word. Return to the store when they have calmed down.

If You Say It, Mean It, and If You Mean It, Follow Through

SAYING WHAT YOU mean and meaning what you say are another extension, or twist, on following through with kind and firm action with your mouth shut. (As you can see, many of these tools can be combined or interchanged for appropriate application.)

When your children get out of bed after their bedtime, kindly and firmly take their hand and lead them back to bed. You might kiss them on the cheek as you put them in bed, but do not say a word. Do this as long as it takes them to realize that when you say, "It is time for bed," you mean it, and when you mean it, you will follow through.

When you have told your children you will not drive while they are fighting, pull over to the side of the road the minute they start fighting. Do not lecture or say a word. Read a magazine until they stop fighting. Do this consistently and they will soon know that you mean what you say and that you will follow through with kindness and firmness.

Less Is More

TO BE EFFECTIVE, remember two things:

1. Less is more. The less you talk, the more effective you will be.
2. Let your actions speak louder than words.

These five tools are all other names for logical consequences, yet they are less likely to be misused as punishment. Of course, anything can be misused if the basic concept is misunderstood.

The Feeling Behind What You Do Is More Important Than What You Do

THE FEELING BEHIND what we do makes all the difference as to whether time-out will be perceived as a punishment or a consequence, whether it is encouraging or discouraging, whether it is effective or ineffective for children in the long run.

One mother reported that time-out "never works for me." Her way of using time-out had been to confine her strong-willed toddler to a time-out chair, with an egg timer ticking away one minute for each year of his age. Her son, outraged at his confinement, resorted to tossing everything within reach at his frazzled mother and struggling relentlessly to get free.

This mother noticed an obvious improvement when she asked with dignity and respect, "Would it help you to go to your feel-good place by yourself, or do you want me to go with you? You can come out as soon as you're ready to do better." The power struggle ended because Mom was no longer hooked into it. Time-out became an effective way for both mother and son to feel better.

One school district found that the main reason it had such a negative school climate was because the staff was enforcing logical consequences with humiliation and put-downs: "You sit on the time-out bench and think about how disrespectful you've been. You've lost the privilege of using the playground for two days."

The staff reported that the school climate changed when they used positive time-out with dignity and respect: "I'm sorry you're not feeling good enough to be respectful to yourself and others. You may sit on the feel-good bench until you feel better. Join us as soon as you know you're ready."

So there we are again. It may need to be said a thousand times before we remember: Children *do* better when they *feel* better. When adults remember this, they will not misuse logical consequences or time-out.

8

Button, Button, Who's Got the Button?

Positive Time-Out for Adults

W E   A L L   H A V E buttons, and children know what they are and how to push them. When our buttons are pushed, we revert to our primitive brain (fight or flight) and "lose it." Everything we "know" evaporates into the ether. While in this state of mind, we don't remember to use positive time-out or any other positive-discipline method. We usually go on a rampage that puts children into their primitive brain where their only option is fight or flight. And into the war zone we go. Power struggles between adults and children seem to be epidemic.

What to Do

I   H O P E   T H E following steps will help you recognize what you are doing a little faster so you can take some positive time-out for yourself until you feel better—until you have access to your cortex and rational behavior. After all, if we expect children to behave rationally, wouldn't it be nice (and effective) if we learned to do it first?

The first thing to do is to forgive yourself (remember that mistakes are wonderful opportunities to learn) and then come up with a plan to do better. What an exceptional example to give your children, who have many mistakes ahead of them in their lifetimes.

> If we expect children to behave rationally, wouldn't it be nice (and effective) if we learned to do it first?

The second thing to remember is that it is unlikely that you will ever be a perfect parent, nor will your children ever be perfect children. "Losing it" is an ongoing process, which is just one reason to learn the valuable skill of taking some positive time-out as soon as you can catch yourself "losing it"—sometimes sooner, and sometimes later. We will *all* continue to make mistakes throughout our lifetimes, even when we know better. By using positive time-out, we can at least learn to manage our behavior until we can crawl out of our reptilian brain and blossom into our cortex where we can think clearly and calmly.

Positive Time-Out for Anger Management

MOST PARENTS FIND it difficult to think clearly and calmly when they or their children are on a rampage. Many parents in parenting classes have the same questions: How do I control my anger? How do I teach my children to control their anger? Is anger wrong? When the stress piles up and my children choose exactly the wrong moment to push my buttons, how do I keep from exploding?

> Most parents find it difficult to think clearly and calmly when they or their children are on a rampage.

We all feel angry from time to time, and many times our anger is understandable or even justified. Sometimes our children's anger is justified, too. But uncontrolled anger can be destructive and can lead us to do and say things we later regret.

Many therapists encourage adults—and children—to observe and become aware of the symptoms of approaching anger and to use time-out as a way of calming down before anger gets out of control. Sometimes we adults need time-out far more than our children do. One of the saddest things to observe is a child being blamed for problems that are caused by adults. How often do adults fail to take responsibility for their part in the behavior? Look around, and you will see it happen too often.

The point is not to make adults feel guilty or to cast blame on them. I would like to repeat, "All people (adults and children) *lose it* at times." The point is that adults are adults and need to take the lead in learning to deal with the ongoing process of "losing it" so they can model these skills for children.

Take Positive Time-Out to Control Your Behavior

ARE YOU AN actor or a reactor? When you feel provoked by a child, do you immediately react to the provocation and impose

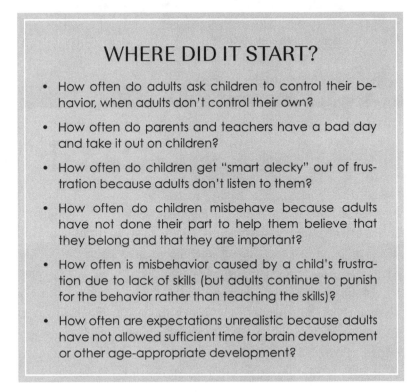

WHERE DID IT START?

- How often do adults ask children to control their behavior, when adults don't control their own?

- How often do parents and teachers have a bad day and take it out on children?

- How often do children get "smart alecky" out of frustration because adults don't listen to them?

- How often do children misbehave because adults have not done their part to help them believe that they belong and that they are important?

- How often is misbehavior caused by a child's frustration due to lack of skills (but adults continue to punish for the behavior rather than teaching the skills)?

- How often are expectations unrealistic because adults have not allowed sufficient time for brain development or other age-appropriate development?

punishment (blame, shame, or pain, often in the form of punitive time-out)? Or do you take time to gain self-control before asking a child to use self-control?

How can children be expected to control behavior when they never see examples of what that control looks like? Having "buttons" is not the problem; losing control when those buttons are pushed is. If we want our children to learn self-control, we must give them a model for this behavior. There are many ways to model time-out for self-control.

Share Your Feelings with an Honest "I" Message

TAKE TIME-OUT TO model that it is okay to feel what you feel and to share your feelings. Sometimes it is appropriate to say, "I'm very upset right now."

POSITIVE TIME-OUT METHODS FOR ANGER MANAGEMENT

Take time out to:

1. Share your feelings with an honest "I" message.

2. Let children know you need to gain self-control.

3. Look at your responsibility in creating the problem.

4. Listen to a child's point of view.

5. Get into a child's world.

6. Be respectful.

7. Study child development.

8. Learn effective discipline skills.

9. Enjoy children.

Whenever Mrs. Kenniwick had a down day, she would inform her students, "I'm having a bad day today. I'll probably feel better tomorrow. Meanwhile, I would really appreciate your support." The students would respond by being extra careful. If one group of students got too noisy, another student would remind them, "Please be more quiet. Mrs. K is having a bad day." The noisy group would immediately settle down.

Let Children Know You Need to Gain Self-Control

THIS IS SIMILAR to sharing feelings with an "I" message; however, it goes beyond sharing your feelings. It also acknowledges the need to take time-out before rational thought can take place. For example, "I'm going to postpone our discussion about this until I can calm down."

Take time-out by going for a walk, listening to music, taking a shower, sitting and reading for awhile, counting to 10, 20, or 100, meditating. Let children know what helps you calm down and feel better so you can deal with a situation rationally.

Look at Your Responsibility in Creating the Problem

MY SIGNATURE STORY (the one I tell in every lecture and in many of my books) is about the time I lost it and called my then eight-year-old daughter, Mary, a spoiled brat. This was obviously a reptilian-brain reaction. (After all, reptiles often eat their young.) Mary stormed off to her room and got even from her reptilian brain. When I calmed down enough to apologize, I went to her room and found her with a copy of my first book, *Positive Discipline,* and a big, black marking pen. She was angrily underlining passages that illustrated how I was not practicing what I preach.

I left her room feeling very sad about how I had blown it. However, it was not long before Mary came out of her room, gave me a big hug, and said, "I'm sorry." This is when I took responsibility for my part in creating the problem. "*I'm* sorry. When I called you a spoiled brat, I was upset at you for losing

> Let children know what helps you calm down and feel better so you can deal with a situation rationally.

control of your behavior. But, I had totally lost control of my own behavior."

Mary followed my model of responsibility and said, "That's okay, Mom. I *was* acting like a spoiled brat."

I continued to take responsibility for my part, "Yes, but I can see how I provoked you to behave that way."

She said, "Yes, but I can see that I. . . ."

We were soon laughing and hugging each other. We then worked together on a way to avoid a similar problem in the future. I can't even remember now the problem or the solution, which illustrates how unimportant most of the problems are over which we lose it.

Listen to a Child's Point of View

MRS. COTTER WAS making school lunches for her seven-year-old son, Sheldon. Sheldon said, "Mom, I won't eat a ham sandwich. Let me make my own cheese sandwich."

Mom said, "I'm making these sandwiches, and you'd better eat them."

Sheldon said, "Well, I won't."

Mrs. Cotter said, "Sheldon, I'm tired of your attitude. You are in time-out."

Sheldon stalked off and said, "Fine, but I won't eat the sandwich."

Mrs. Cotter made several mistakes. First, she should have encouraged Sheldon to make his own sandwiches in order to help him develop perceptions of capability. Of course, he would need time for training and some joint decision making to make sure he would include healthy foods. Second, she should have listened to Sheldon and engaged him in a conversation about his dislike of ham. She could have then shown appreciation for his willingness to make his own substitute sandwich. Her biggest mistake was accusing Sheldon of having an attitude when her own attitude was very disrespectful.

Get into a Child's World

THIS STEP GOES beyond simply listening to what a child says. Sometimes we have to be perceptive enough to dig beneath the words to understand a child's world.

Eleven-year-old Lisa constantly wore an ugly green windbreaker. She refused to take it off. Her single father thought her behavior was defiant. When she refused his request to take off the jacket, he tried humiliation—letting her know how ugly it was and how much she looked like a boy when she wore it. Although Lisa felt very hurt by this, she covered up her hurt feelings by being more defiant and acting as though she didn't care what he thought. She displayed what adults call "an attitude."

> Sometimes we have to be perceptive enough to dig beneath the words to understand a child's world.

If Dad had taken time-out to get into Lisa's world, he would have learned that she had a reason for wearing the ugly green jacket. Lisa was developing breasts and felt embarrassed. She wore the jacket to cover up her embarrassment. She also felt very sad and hurt because she didn't have a mother to talk to about this "problem." Her hurt feelings gave her even more incentive to take it out on her Dad. Instead of dealing with the real problem, Dad kept creating a power struggle, in which Lisa was a formidable foe.

One night her father hid the jacket while Lisa was sleeping. She refused to go to school the next day. Dad thought she was being stubborn and disrespectful. Lisa was just trying to protect herself from her perceived embarrassment. Dad didn't understand that he was creating this power struggle, which he was losing. Dad escalated the power struggle to a revenge cycle by grounding Lisa (a very negative form of time-out). Lisa said, "Fine," and plopped herself on the couch in front of the TV.

After two days, Dad relented a little. He told Lisa she had to go to school and gave her back the jacket. However, he tried to maintain some control and told her she could not leave the house, except to go to school, until she was ready to wear something other than the green jacket. Lisa said, "I won't go to school if I can't go anywhere else."

Dad finally gave up saying, "I can't understand your behavior. Where did I go wrong?" Lisa felt his anger and discouragement. This made her feel guilty, but she couldn't give up the jacket. She had a reason for wearing it.

All the power struggles and revenge cycles (that were blamed on Lisa) were created because Dad did not take time-out to get into Lisa's world to find out was going on for her. How could grounding (punitive time-out) possibly solve this problem?

In Chapter 5, we discussed many implications of understanding the Four Mistaken Goals of Behavior. Here, the point is the importance of adults taking time-out to get into the child's world.

Be Respectful

WHEN YOU CAN see that a child has lost it and needs time to calm down, you might lead him or her to a positive time-out area and say, "Let me know when you have taken time to calm down, and I'll let you know when I have calmed down. When we are both ready, we will work together to find a solution." Another possibility is to ask, "Would you like to put this problem on the family/class meeting agenda or should I? By the time it comes up in our meeting we will feel better and can focus on solutions."

Children can feel the energy of your attitude. If you are respectful, they are more likely to respond in kind.

One principal shared that he finds it very respectful (and effective) to take a misbehaving child for a walk as one way to use positive time-out. He finds that this creates a cooling-off period and helps to build a foundation of trust and good feelings, which is necessary for change to take place. A child treated in a caring and respectful manner has less incentive to misbehave.

Children can feel the energy of your attitude. If you are respectful, they are more likely to respond in kind. If they can't, it could be that they haven't had time to access their cortex. Until then, they can't behave respectfully. Have faith that they will as soon as they are able.

Study Child Development

IN CHAPTER 3, I discussed the developmental reasons why even positive time-out is usually not effective for children under the age of three. Some parents get angry when small children spill milk or juice, rather than realizing their little fingers are not always capable of the coordination necessary to avoid spilling large containers. Some teachers expect children to sit for longer periods of time than what is appropriate for their age or temperament. (For more information about temperament, see *Positive Discipline: The First Three Years* [Nelson, Erwin, and Duffy, 1998] and *Positive Discipline for Preschoolers* [Nelsen, Erwin, and Duffy, 1998].) Adults forget (or don't know) that temper tantrums often are the only recourse children have when they have not yet learned delayed gratification and/or socially acceptable ways to achieve their goals.

Many children have not learned the difference between wants and needs. Parents usually give their children too many things and then are surprised that they have taught materialism instead of gratitude. Children are constantly bombarded with television commercials designed to make them want so many things, which only reinforces materialism instead of gratitude. Then when these children misbehave by demanding things *now*, adults forget that part of the problem is developmental and part of the problem was created by the parents.

Parents and children will benefit considerably when the parents understand child development issues. The rest can be handled through effective discipline skills.

Learn Effective Discipline Skills

YOU ARE ALREADY doing this by reading this book. Congratulations. Too many parents forget that training is required for any worthy endeavor. They would not consider being a bricklayer or a brain surgeon without training. Yet they often think they are being wise to engage in the most important job of all—parenting—without any training at all in effective discipline. Of course, learning these skills is complicated by the fact that so many parenting "experts" teach conflicting methods.

An important part of taking time to learn effective discipline skills is to trust your own heart and common sense. Once you have taken the time to get into the child's world and to understand the long-range results, you will disregard any discipline methods that are not respectful to the child and that do not teach important life skills.

Enjoy Children

THIS IS THE most important time-out of all. Most parents have children because they want to enjoy them. Most teachers get into education because they love working with children. Too often the goal of taking time to enjoy children becomes lost. Parents get too busy in their lives. Teachers feel overwhelmed with "false" goals of education. We live in a fast-paced world where we often get our priorities confused. We say our children are what we value most, yet we spend our time and energy pursuing other goals, leaving our children feeling neglected and misunderstood.

> We say our children are what we value most, yet we spend our time and energy pursuing other goals, leaving our children feeling neglected and misunderstood.

What greater feeling could children experience in their lives than knowing that their parents and teachers enjoy them? If all children experienced this, they would feel belonging and significance, which would eliminate the need to misbehave. Take time-out to enjoy your children!

9

Attitude Tools for Avoiding Power Struggles While Empowering Children

A QUESTION THAT needs to be answered is, What causes power struggles between adults and children in the first place? There are many causes, including plain old crankiness (in both children and adults) from being too tired or being in a bad mood. Some power struggles are embedded in developmental issues. In other words, children are in a continuing process of individuating—finding out who they are and what they can do separate from their parents. Many power struggles occur because both children and adults lack skills to get their needs met.

Using positive time-out to get adults and children through the crankiness issues probably seems obvious. Less obvious is

> ## THREE BASIC NEEDS OF CHILDREN
>
> **1.** Sense of belonging and significance
> **2.** Personal power and autonomy
> **3.** Life skills (social skills and problem-solving skills) for success

how to diminish other reasons for power struggles. Understanding some basic needs of children and learning the skills to empower children to meet those needs will significantly end the need for even positive time-out.

When children do not believe they belong and are significant (see Chapter 5), they often use destructive methods in their misguided attempt to meet this need. When adults are too controlling, children do not have an opportunity to express their personal power and autonomy in constructive ways. So, they choose destructive ways (power struggles). All of the positive-discipline methods are designed to teach children the social and problem-solving skills they need to be successful in life.

Squelching the Basic Needs of Children

ONE OF THE biggest mistakes made by parents and teachers is not recognizing the need of children to have power and autonomy in their lives. This mistake is then followed by the mistake of not taking the time to provide children with opportunities to use their power and autonomy in constructive ways.

It requires a huge paradigm shift for adults to stop thinking that they should control children for their own good or for expediency. Yes, it is easier for adults to have children who sit in neat little rows and obediently do what they are told. At least it used to be easy—when children were more likely to go along with this. However, there are few children today who will not rebel and engage in power struggles when adults try to use power over them.

O ne of the biggest mistakes made by parents and teachers is not recognizing the need of children to have power and autonomy in their lives.

The Foundation for Avoiding Power Struggles

YOU MAY HAVE noticed that a key ingredient for most positive-discipline methods is getting children involved. Involving children in the discipline process meets all three of the basic needs of children.

Tools for Avoiding Power Struggles

MANY, BUT NOT all, of the nonpunitive discipline tools presented in this chapter have been discussed throughout this book and in other *Positive Discipline* books.[1] This chapter and

1. *Positive Discipline* (Nelsen, 1996); *Positive Discipline A–Z* (Nelsen, Lott, and Glenn, 1999); *Positive Discipline: The First Three Years* (Nelsen, Erwin, and Duffy, 1998); *Positive Discipline for Preschoolers* (Nelsen, Erwin, and Duffy, 1998); *Positive Discipline for Teenagers*, rev. ed. (Nelsen and Lott, 2000); *Positive Discipline for Single Parents*, 2nd ed. (Nelsen, Erwin, and Delzer, 1999); *Positive Discipline for Blended Families* (Nelsen, Erwin, and Glenn, 1997); *Positive Discipline for Parenting in Recovery* (Nelsen, Lott, and Intner, 1996); *Positive Discipline in the Classroom*, rev. ed. (Nelsen, Lott, and Glenn, 2000); *Positive Discipline: A Teacher's A–Z Guide* (Nelsen, Duffy, Escobar, Ortolano, and Owen-Sohocki, 1996).

You may have noticed that a key ingredient for most positive-discipline methods is getting children involved.

the next will serve as a handy summary of the many possible ways to avoid power struggles while empowering children.

It is important to remember that positive time-out is not the only discipline tool and is not always appropriate. Some of the following discipline tools could be used in place of positive time-out. Others (such as exploring through what and how questions) will be more effective after both children and adults take a positive time-out and are in a rational state of mind.

These discipline tools are listed under two categories: Attitude Tools (in this chapter) and Action Tools (in the next chapter). All are based on the following criteria:

CRITERIA FOR POSITIVE-DISCIPLINE TOOLS

1. They are based on kindness, firmness, dignity, and respect.

2. They all consider the long-range results.

3. They all teach children important life skills for success.

Attitude Tools

ADULTS HAVE THE major responsibility for creating an encouraging environment, although children also play a part.

We must learn to control our behavior before we can expect children to control their own behavior. Sometimes adults need to take some positive time-out until they can adopt encouraging attitudes.

Dealing with children who are having temper tantrums or are being defiant in any way is enough to challenge any adult. However, we must remember that they are children and we are adults. We must learn to control our behavior before we can expect children to control their own behavior. Sometimes adults need to take some positive time-out until they can adopt encouraging attitudes.

The feeling behind what you do is more important than what you do. "I love you" can be said in an unbelievable tone of voice as well as a believable one. Attitude is the key. When you are struggling to create an encouraging environment, take time to read over the attitude tools for inspiration (listed in the box on page 120). They could be used as daily affirmations.

Misbehaving Children Are Discouraged Children

CHAPTER 5 IS devoted to this important fact of human behavior. Yet, it can be difficult for any adult to remember that a child who is misbehaving is really saying, "I'm a child, and I just want to belong." The related action tool (Action Tool 20, discussed in Chapter 10) is to get into the child's world to deal with the belief behind the behavior.

Children *Do* Better When They *Feel* Better

WHERE DID WE ever get the crazy idea that in order to get children to do better, we first have to make them feel worse?

We will not be effective with children until we incorporate this important truth into our basic philosophy of what discipline is all about. Many adults seem to be brainwashed with the idea that children have to suffer (and pay for what they did) before they can learn. There are many action tools related to this attitude, only one of which is creating positive time-out for children to feel better so they can do better.

Mistakes Are Wonderful Opportunities to Learn

SO MUCH MISERY could be eliminated if we would incorporate this fact into our innermost beings. We could eliminate

FOURTEEN ATTITUDE TOOLS

1. Misbehaving children are discouraged children.

2. Children *do* better when they *feel* better.

3. Mistakes are wonderful opportunities to learn.

4. Work for improvement, not perfection.

5. Use kindness and firmness at the same time.

6. Focus on winning children over instead of winning over children.

7. Focus on long-range results.

8. Look for solutions, not blame.

9. Understand the meaning of discipline.

10. Treat children with dignity and respect.

11. Children listen to you *after* they feel listened to.

12. Look for the hidden message behind misbehavior.

13. Give children the benefit of the doubt.

14. Lighten up—breathe.

the disease of perfectionism. We could eliminate so much blame, shame, and pain. We could create a safe learning environment. We could help children be excited about the possibility of learning from mistakes instead of freezing in fear and self-doubt.

The following quotes are filled with the wisdom of using mistakes as learning opportunities.

"The greatest mistake one can make in life is to be continually fearing that you will make one."

—*Elbert Hubbard*

"If at first you don't succeed, you are running about average."

—*M. H. Alderson*

"Look at what you have left, never look at what you have lost."

—*Robert Schuller*

"The person who is incapable of making a mistake is incapable of anything."

—*Abraham Lincoln*

Edison was once chided, "It is too bad you had so many failures before you were successful." Edison replied, "I didn't have failures. I learned many things that did not work."

Work for Improvement, Not Perfection

I HAVE OFTEN thought that I would become a basket case if someone followed me around correcting me every time I made a mistake. It would be even worse if I was punished for these mistakes. Yet isn't this what many adults do with children? It would be much more encouraging if someone followed me around saying things such as, "Wow, I'll bet you learn a lot from that experience. You are improving every day. Keep it up."

Sometimes children make mistakes over and over as they improve. Fortunately, little children have no concept of *mistake* when they fall down while learning to walk. They don't waste any time thinking about their fall. How could they possibly improve if they wasted time thinking, "Oh, I failed. What will people think? I'd better be more careful so I don't humiliate myself." Instead, they jump up (sometimes after a little cry) and go about the job of improving their walking skills.

Use Kindness and Firmness at the Same Time

SOMETIMES ADULTS WHO are against punishment go to the other extreme and become permissive. This will not happen if you remember to be both kind and firm at the same time. One related action tool is "I love you, and the answer is no." Another related action tool is to shut your mouth and act—with a kind and firm attitude.

Focus on Winning Children Over Instead of Winning Over Children

MANY ADULTS DON'T think about the fact that if they win the power struggles with their children, that makes their children "the losers." Ask yourself, "Am I being empowering or discouraging to my child?"

Focus on Long-Range Results

ONE OF THE main criteria for every discipline method we use should be to consider what our children are learning from the experience. Are they learning communication skills, problem-solving skills, social interest? Or are they learning that the one who has the most power can treat others disrespectfully?

Look for Solutions, Not Blame

WHEN WE ARE upset, we often seek blame instead of solutions. Then what? When tempted to look for blame, take some time-out until you can think and behave more rationally.

Understand the Meaning of Discipline

AS STATED IN Chapter 1, *discipline* comes from the Latin word *disipulus,* meaning "pupil," and *disciplina,* meaning "to teach or educate." People often think that positive discipline is an oxymoron, because they think of punishment and discipline as synonymous. But these two ideas are not synonymous. When we understand the true meaning of discipline, we will use methods that teach or that inspire children to become followers of truth and principle.

Treat Children with Dignity and Respect

YOU WILL NOTICE that most positive-discipline tools are based on universal principles. Everyone—including children—wants to be treated with dignity and respect. People do better when they feel better. People need to learn the life skills of social interest. We all need to feel that we belong and are significant.

Children Listen to You *After* They Feel Listened To

I GET SUCH a kick out of this one. Whenever adults complain that children don't listen, I can guess with 100 percent accuracy that they have not listened to the child. So much of what adults do is based on "non-thinking." We do so many things that just don't make sense. How can children learn to listen when they don't have a model of what listening is about? How can they listen when they are put on the defensive? No one listens when they feel threatened; they move into their primitive brain. It is up to adults to create an atmosphere where children can listen.

Look for the Hidden Message Behind Misbehavior

IT WILL TAKE practice to look at a misbehaving child and see a child who is saying, "Notice me. Involve me." or "Let me help. Give me choices." or "I'm hurting. Validate my feelings." or "Have faith in me. Show me a small step." You might want to read Chapter 5 several times to absorb this valuable tool. Many parents and teachers keep a copy of the Mistaken Goal Chart on their refrigerators or desks.

Give Children the Benefit of the Doubt

WHAT A DIFFERENCE it would make if we assumed the best about children instead of the worst. What if we assumed they had a good reason for doing what they did, and then checked it out with them? In other words, wouldn't it be wonderful if children knew we were "on their side"? It would also be helpful and respectful if we had more faith in the abilities of children—to know that they can solve many problems on their own, that they can survive difficult feelings and disappointments without being rescued or overprotected. We also need to remember that what they do today is not an indicator of who they will be when they grow up. Most of all, we need to respect their right to be who they are and to learn their life lessons (with our loving, guiding support) in their own time and in their own way.

Lighten Up—Breathe

YOU MAY NEED to take some positive time-out to do this. If you do, you will scc things much differently, more positively, more lovingly.

The action tools presented in the next chapter are effective only when adults adopt the attitudes described in this chapter. The preceding fourteen attitudes are the foundation for the encouragement of children.

10

Action Tools for Avoiding Power Struggles While Empowering Children

I T CAN BE very difficult to change old discipline patterns—even when they don't work. It helps to learn effective discipline skills to replace the old patterns. This, however, is not as easy as it may sound. Getting rid of old patterns and applying new skills requires a paradigm shift; adults really have to see themselves and their children differently. This fact became evident to me during my parenting lectures. During each lecture, I create long lists of specific kind and firm discipline tools, and I hang these lists on the classroom walls. During the question-and-answer period, however, parents inevitably ask, "But what do I do about such-and-such?" I inwardly groan and think, "Don't they see that there are at least six parenting tools out of the many listed on the walls that would be very effective for the situation described?" Of course, I can't say this out loud, but it always makes me wonder, "Why don't they get it?"

I think I have a possible answer: Many parents are asking the wrong questions. As long as adults ask questions similar to the following, kind and firm discipline may not fit into their paradigm.

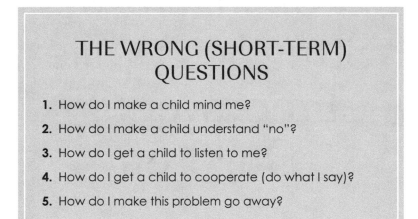

THE WRONG (SHORT-TERM) QUESTIONS

1. How do I make a child mind me?

2. How do I make a child understand "no"?

3. How do I get a child to listen to me?

4. How do I get a child to cooperate (do what I say)?

5. How do I make this problem go away?

You may be thinking that there isn't anything wrong with any of these questions. They may seem perfectly legitimate to you. If so, you are in short-term discipline mentality (thinking in terms of what works in the moment). If, instead, "the right" questions (on the following page) become your point of reference, you will shift to a long-range discipline mentality (thinking in terms of long-range results for children).

Adopt the "Right" Questions

DON'T THE LONG-RANGE questions represent what you truly want? The interesting thing about these questions is that when they are answered, there will be no need for the "wrong" questions. If children are respectfully involved in the problem-solving process, they still may not mind you (which isn't really healthy anyway), but they will be more likely to cooperate. If children feel listened to by an adult who has learned the skills that invite listening, they will be more likely to listen in turn.

THE RIGHT (LONG-RANGE) QUESTIONS

1. How do I help a child become capable?

2. How do I get into a child's world and support his or her developmental process?

3. How do I help a child feel belonging and significance by listening?

4. How do I help a child learn social and life (cooperation) skills, such as communication and problem solving?

5. How do I use this problem as an opportunity for learning—for children and for myself?

Yes, children will make mistakes. Yes, it will be hard to watch them make mistakes, especially big ones. But remember, the freedom to make mistakes and learn from them is essential to a healthy growth process. Can you think of one person you really admire who has not made some big mistakes in life? No. Making mistakes is an essential part of living that children must learn about. It's incredible how much time and energy parents waste by trying to save their children from making mistakes. What a gift it would be for you and your children to see problems and mistakes as opportunities to learn—a situation that is much more empowering than seeing them as stumbling blocks.

FORTY-ONE ACTION TOOLS

1. Be sure the message of love and respect gets through.
2. Allow children to develop the Significant Seven Perceptions and Skills.
3. Don't do things for children that they can do for themselves.
4. Ask what and how questions.
5. Ask curiosity questions.
6. Get children involved in solutions.
7. Hold regular family or class meetings.
8. Use one-on-one problem solving.
9. Establish problem-solving guidelines.
10. Create routines *with* children.
11. Offer limited choices.
12. Redirect misguided power.
13. Say "I notice."
14. Focus on solutions.
15. Create a "Wheel of Choice."
16. Use emotional honesty.
17. Teach the difference between what children feel and what they do.
18. Take responsibility for your part in the conflict.
19. Give children a timer to set for themselves.
20. Get into the child's world.

Action Tools

AS YOU BECOME familiar with the forty-one action tools, you will notice that many of them work better when combined with or after using another tool. And, of course, they will be

21. Use reflective listening.

22. Use active listening.

23. Supervise, supervise, supervise.

24. Distract and/or redirect.

25. Use the Four Rs for Recovery from Mistakes.

26. Stay out of fights.

27. Put children in the same boat.

28. Take time to train.

29. Decide what you will do.

30. Follow through.

31. Less is more.

32. Use nonverbal signals.

33. Say, "As soon as _____, then _____."

34. Teach natural consequences.

35. Teach logical consequences.

36. Use encouragement instead of praise or rewards.

37. Allowances are not related to chores.

38. Get children involved in chores.

39. Give hugs.

40. Provide special time.

41. Use positive time-out.

more effective when combined with any one of the attitude tools from Chapter 9. Most of the action tools have been discussed in other *Positive Discipline* books. This chapter simply provides a handy summary.

None of the tools works all the time for every problem and with every child. Whenever you find yourself involved in a power struggle or in any kind of conflict with your children, take some time-out to go over these tools and the attitude tools. One or several will seem just right for you and for your children. Your heart will lead you to the tools that will help.

Be Sure the Message of Love and Respect Gets Through

YOU KNOW YOU love your child, but does your child know it? One child responded, when asked, "I know you love me if I am good." A teenager replied, "Sure, I know you love me if I get good grades." It takes thought and listening to the child to make sure the unconditional message of love gets through.

It is not easy to love a child who is behaving obnoxiously. However, this child is the most in need of love. Remember that a misbehaving child is a discouraged child. It can be very effective to interrupt whatever is going on by saying, "Do you know I really love you?" Some teachers prefer, "Do you know I really care about you?" As Carter Bayton, a successful inner-city schoolteacher said, "You have to reach the heart before you can reach the head."

It is important to understand that love does not mean doing too much for your child. (See Action Tool 3.) Sometimes the most loving thing you can do is respect a child's ability to handle struggles, frustrations, disappointment, and other life situations that provide opportunities for learning and developing perceptions of capability.

Allow Children to Develop the Significant Seven Perceptions and Skills

MOST IMPORTANT LIFE skills would fit under the following seven headings. Positive-discipline tools are designed to help children develop the Significant Seven Perceptions and Skills (Glenn and Nelsen, 1987).

As discussed in Chapter 9, one of the best ways to help children develop is through their respectful involvement. Family and class meetings (Action Tool 7) also provide an excellent opportunity for children to learn all of the Significant Seven Perceptions and Skills.

THE SIGNIFICANT SEVEN PERCEPTIONS AND SKILLS

Perceptions of personal capability
"I am capable."

Perceptions of significance in primary relationships
"I can contribute in meaningful ways. I am genuinely needed."

Perceptions of personal power of influence over life
"I have personal power and influence in my life."

Intrapersonal skills
"I have the ability to understand my personal emotions and to use that understanding to develop self-discipline and self-control."

Interpersonal skills
"I have the ability to work with others, and I can develop friendships through communicating, cooperating, negotiating, sharing, empathizing, and listening."

Systemic skills
"I have the ability to respond to the limits and consequences of everyday life with responsibility, adaptability, flexibility, and integrity."

Judgment skills
"I have the ability to use wisdom and to evaluate situations according to appropriate values."

Don't Do Things for Children that They Can Do for Themselves

TOO MANY PARENTS are doing things like dressing their children in the morning. They do this to save time and because their children look better. Which is more important: expediency and looking good for the neighbors, or making sure children feel capable and competent? Parents need to realize that when they dress their children, they are robbing them of the opportunity to develop strength in perceptions of capability. It is better to take time for training (Action Tool 28), create a morning routine (Action Tool 10), and then get up a few minutes earlier in the morning. You might also train children how to set their own alarm clocks.

In the classroom, bulletin boards may look very professional when teachers create them. However, this helps the teacher, not the students, feel capable. Help your students feel capable and competent by letting them design their own bulletin boards, job charts, and so on.

Ask What and How Questions

TOO MANY PARENTS and teachers tell children what happened, what caused it to happen, how the children should feel

Which is more important: expediency and looking good for the neighbors, or making sure children feel capable and competent?

about it, and what they should do about it. This does not engage children in thinking and problem-solving skills; it creates defensiveness and power struggles. Every time you are tempted to *tell*, stop and, with the true intent of helping your child learn from within, ask:

What happened?

What were you trying to accomplish?

How do you feel about what happened?

What did you learn from this experience?

How can you use what you learned in the future?

What ideas do you have to take care of the problem now?

What and how questions are not effective during a time of conflict. Allow time for you and your child to be in your rational brains before using the preceding questions. These questions and the time-out will help your children think for themselves.

Several school principals ask children to answer these questions on paper before talking with them. They find this serves as a positive time-out and gives the children time to explore, for themselves, before discussing situations with the principal.

Ask Curiosity Questions

WHEN CHILDREN DO something, avoid the temptation to defend yourself, explain yourself, give a lecture about how they should feel differently, or solve their problem. You can help your child explore deeper feelings by asking, "Can you tell me more about that? Could you give me an example? Is there anything else you want to say about that? Anything else?" You may ask, "Anything else?" several times before your child can't think of anything else. Trust your instincts about where to go from here. It could be that your child feels satisfied to have a sounding board. You could ask, "Would you like my help to brainstorm possibilities?" Avoid the temptation to help if your child doesn't ask for your help.

Get Children Involved in Solutions

THIS IS ONE of the themes that is presented over and over in this book because it is one of the things adults often fail to do. Why? Because it seems more expedient and efficient for adults to give edicts instead of getting children involved. I say "*seems more expedient and efficient*" because it is an illusion. What may seem expedient for the moment is lost in the long term if the edicts have to be repeated over and over because children haven't learned life skills and cooperation through involvement. The cost of efficiency is just too great when the price is not only lack of skill building for children, but also resentment

and rebellion when they experience lack of respect and too much control from adults.

When children are involved in solutions to problems that they face in their families or classrooms, they have a feeling of ownership and an incentive to follow plans they help create. There are several ways to encourage young people to be involved in solving problems: use one-on-one problem solving between teacher and student, parent and child, or two children; or organize and hold regular family or class meetings.

Hold Regular Family or Class Meetings

ONE OF THE most powerful tools available for solving problems, communicating in an encouraging and positive way, and learning social interest is the family or class meeting. These meetings provide a format for children to learn, by experience, problem-solving skills, respect for differences, and so many other ingredients that lead to a sense of belonging and significance.

Family or class meetings teach children and adults to help each other with positive solutions, rather than hurt each other with blame and punitive methods. If parents and teachers understood the value of this process, they couldn't claim they didn't have time for it any more than they could say they don't have time to teach reading and math.

Use One-on-One Problem Solving

AS AN ELEMENTARY school counselor, I learned the value of getting students involved in solutions. (It is fairly easy to see how the same ideas could be applied to siblings or to fights among friends.)

Students would often be sent to my office for fighting. In the beginning, I would make the mistake of trying to help them solve their fights by listening to their stories and coming up with suggestions for solutions. They always argued with my suggestions; they wanted me to take sides. (Remember that rivalries or arguments between children are often designed to win power or adult attention.)

Family or class meetings teach children and adults to help each other with positive solutions, rather than hurt each other with blame and punitive methods.

I decided to leave the counseling office and let the two students work things out themselves based on one rule: Forget about blame, and work on solutions. I told them to come out and let me know their plan for solutions as soon as they had worked it out. I was amazed at how quickly they could work things out when I would leave them alone with that one rule.

When I stayed in the office, we could talk for ten minutes and the kids would seem angrier than ever and not have any solutions. The first time I left two kids alone to work things out, they were finished in about two minutes. One student agreed to give his opponent one of his t-shirts because his had been ripped in the fight. The other student agreed that he would let his opponent get ahead of him in the lunch line for a week because he had crowded in front and started the fight.

Establish Problem-Solving Guidelines

THE FOLLOWING GUIDELINES for solving problems are adapted from *Positive Discipline* (Nelsen, 1996). These guidelines allow you to work with others to settle disagreements and resolve problems in a healthy, positive way. Parents and teachers should become familiar with the steps and practice them with young people so everyone is comfortable with them *before* conflict arises.

1. Ignore the provocation. (It takes more courage to walk away than to stay and fight.)

    a. Do something else. (Find another game or activity.)
    b. Leave long enough for a cooling-off period (positive time-out), then settle it.

2. Talk it over respectfully.

    a. Tell the other person how you feel. Let him or her know you don't like what is happening.
    b. Listen without interrupting to what the other person has to say about how he or she feels and what he or she doesn't like.
    c. Take turns sharing what each of you thinks you did to contribute to the problem.
    d. Take turns sharing what each of you is willing to do differently.
    e. Brainstorm other possible solutions.

3. Choose a solution or solutions you can both agree on from 2d and 2e above.

4. If you just can't work it out together, ask for help.

    a. Put it on the family- or class-meeting agenda.
    b. Talk it over with a parent, teacher, or friend.

Create Routines *with* Children

THE CREATION OF routine charts *with* children is one of the best ways to avoid power struggles while empowering children. (There's that word again: *with*.) Sit down with your children and brainstorm the items that should go on a routine chart. For example, for a bedtime routine chart, the list might include pick up toys, take bath, put on pajamas, snack, brush

teeth, get things ready for morning, read story, hugs. Of course, while brainstorming, these items will be in any order. Let children decide what the final order should be, although you can provide input and suggestions. For example, if children put brushing teeth before snacks, you may suggest switching the two. Once the final order is decided, have children write the items on a large piece of colored tag paper (or you can write it if your children are not old enough). Then have children cut out and glue pictures from old magazines to represent each item on the routine chart.

The chart now becomes the boss, instead of you or your children. All you have to say is, "What is next on your bedtime routine chart?" When children have been actively involved in the creation of routine charts, they are more willing to follow them.

You and your children can create routine charts for any time when structure will help, such as morning, schoolwork (see Chapter 7), preparation for recess, or preparation for leaving the classroom.

Offer Limited Choices

THIS IS AN excellent way to be both kind and firm: kind because children can use their power to have some choice, firm because the choice is limited. It helps to be creative when giving limited choices. One mother, confronted with a child who was reluctant to pick up his toys, asked, "Do you want to hop like a bunny or slither like a snake while you pick up your toys?" Soon, her son was slithering around the floor, picking up his toys.

Redirect Misguided Power

LET CHILDREN HELP you. Find ways for them to contribute. This might include a choice of two ways to help. Another possibility is to say, "I would appreciate anything you can do to help clean up the room." Many children appreciate the opportunity to use their own creativity, and often do more than when they are given a specific order.

Sometimes you must first redirect your own misguided power. It may be helpful to stop and say, "Whoops. I think we are in a power struggle. I apologize for my part on this. Of course you wouldn't want to help when I boss you around. What ideas do you have that would help us work together respectfully?"

Say "I Notice"

STOP USING SET-UP questions such as "Did you clean your room or do your homework?" when you know they didn't. Instead say, "I notice you didn't do your homework." This might be followed with any or all of the next three tools.

Focus on Solutions

DURING FAMILY OR class meetings or in one-on-one discussions or anytime, you might ask, "What ideas do have for getting your homework done?" or, "Why don't you create a plan that works for you on getting your homework done? You can show it to me tomorrow."

Create a "Wheel of Choice"

(SEE THE SAMPLE Wheel of Choice.) The Wheel of Choice is a favorite for encouraging children to focus on solutions. Sometimes children appreciate a choice, "Which do you think would help you the most right now: taking some positive time-out, putting this problem on the family- or class-meeting agenda, or using the Wheel of Choice?"

Use Emotional Honesty

USING EMOTIONAL HONESTY is an excellent model for children. An important attitude that goes along with this tool is understanding that others may not feel or think the same, and they may not give you what you want. However, it is important for children to know what they think and feel.

Use this formula when talking with children: "I feel _____ about/when _____ because _____ and I wish _____." For example, "I feel worried when you don't do your homework because I know how important it can be to help you be successful in life. I wish you would consider what it could mean to your future if you don't do it."

Teach the Difference Between What Children Feel and What They Do

ONE REASON MANY children do not develop strength in intrapersonal skills of the Significant Seven ("I have the ability to understand my personal emotions and to use that understanding to develop self-discipline and self-control") is that parents and teachers don't allow them to have their feelings. When a child says, "I hate my baby brother," he is told, "No you don't." When a student says, "That teacher was unfair," she is often told, "Well, what did you do?"

It would be more appropriate to say, "I can see that you are very angry at your brother right now, and I can't let you

WHEEL OF CHOICE

hit him." or "Can you tell me more about that, and what it is that seemed unfair to you?" It is important for children to learn that what they feel is always okay, but what they do is a different matter. What they do must be respectful. "Would you like to hit the bop bag or draw a picture about how you feel?"

Take Responsibility for Your Part in the Conflict

I HAVE NEVER seen a power-drunk child without a power-drunk parent or teacher nearby. Most adults don't like to look at their own behavior and admit that they may be too controlling. Most people rebel when they feel controlled.

It can be very helpful to tell children what you have done to create the conflict. This often invites them to look at their part. If you are engaged in many power struggles with your children, you may need to say, "I think I have been trying to control you too much. I don't blame you for resenting this. I would like to start over and work together to find respectful solutions to any problems we have."

Give Children a Timer to Set for Themselves

WHEN CHILDREN RESIST a request to pick up toys, go to bed, or leave the playground, you might give them a timer and ask them to set it for 5 or 10 minutes. Then when the timer goes off, they will know it is time to start their task. This gives them power (though limited) over their fate, and takes you out of the middle. The timer becomes the boss.

Get into the Child's World

DEAL WITH THE belief behind the behavior. You might do this through goal disclosure (see Chapter 5) or through either of the following two tools.

Use Reflective Listening

REFLECTIVE LISTENING MEANS that you reflect what you hear back to your child or student. It is best to use words that are a little different so you don't sound like a parrot. However, stick closely to what the child is saying.

> *Child:* I hate Jody.
> *Parent:* You hate your sister.
> *Child:* Yes, she always takes my things without asking me.
> *Parent:* You feel she violates your privacy.
>
> *Student:* The other kids don't ever pick me for their team.
> *Teacher:* Do you feel angry when you aren't chosen?

Student: Yes. It hurts my feelings.

Teacher. It hurts to be left out.

Through reflective listening, a child is often able to vent and then to come up with a solution. The child in the first dialogue asked for a "do not disturb" sign for her door. Mom agreed that this solution sounded reasonable and that they might also brainstorm for solutions during a family meeting that would include her sister. The student in the second dialogue decided she would put the problem on the class-meeting agenda and ask for help.

Use Active Listening

ACTIVE LISTENING GOES beyond reflective listening. In active listening, you listen for the feelings between the words, which means making guesses that help children feel understood and validated.

Child: I hate Jody.

Parent: You sound furious with your sister.

Child: Yes, she takes my things without asking.

Parent: It sounds like you feel outraged that she could be so disrespectful.

Child (in tears): How could she do that?

Parent: You wonder how anyone could be so thoughtless and inconsiderate.

Child: (Sobs.)

This is the time to stop active listening and just hold her for awhile.

It is important to let children have their feelings without always trying to fix things for them. Later you could ask if she would like some help trying to find a solution.

Supervise, Supervise, Supervise

MANY PARENTS DON'T like the fact that supervision is the primary tool that should be used with children under the age of two to three. Supervision shouldn't stop after these ages. It is just that, as children develop more reasoning capabilities, you can add more tools. The next tool is closely related to supervision.

Distract and/or Redirect

SHOW CHILDREN WHAT they *can* do, instead of always telling them what they *can't* do. "You can play with the Tupperware now." or "You can climb on this toy," instead of on the couch. "It's okay to climb on the jungle gym outside, but not on the desk." or "You can tape some paper to your desk for doodling." Remember that this has to be done over and over and over with small children.

By telling children what they can do, they hear the positive possibilities before they are told what they can't do or before they are physically removed from a dangerous or unacceptable behavior.

Use the Four Rs for Recovery from Mistakes

ONE OF THE attitude tools is to see mistakes as learning opportunities. We can model this tool for children through the Four Rs of Recovery from Mistakes.

1. Recognize (that you made a mistake)
2. Responsibility (take responsibility for your part)
3. Reconcile (say you are sorry)
4. Resolve (work on a solution together)

Most parents and teachers admit that when they apologize to a child, the child is usually very forgiving. In fact, the child usually says, "That's okay, Mom, Dad, Teacher." By apologizing, you create a positive learning environment where it will be effective to work on solutions. It would not be effective to focus on solutions until you have done the first three steps of the Four Rs.

Stay Out of Fights

MOST PARENTS HAVE difficulty understanding that one of the major reasons children fight is to get their parents involved. They often tell me, "That isn't true. My children fight when I'm not around." I ask them how they know. They grin as they say, "Well, they call me up or let me know the minute I walk through the door."

Staying out of fights isn't the only way to deal with them, but it can be an effective way. Let your children know in advance that you will stay out of their fights at the time of conflict and that you will be available at other times (such as during family or class meetings) to help them work on solutions to their conflicts. (If you can't accept this tool, see the next tool.)

Put Children in the Same Boat

IT IS IMPORTANT that you treat all children the same. If you take sides (even though you think you saw what happened and who started it), you engage in victim/bully training. The child who is rescued soon finds he or she can feel special by getting the other one into trouble (without being caught). The one who is blamed feels resentful and angry enough to bully the one who is usually at fault.

There are several ways to put children in the same boat. You can ask them to take the fight outside. You can suggest they go to separate positive time-out areas until they have calmed down and are ready to stop fighting. You can send them to the same positive time-out area to work on a solution together. You can ask who would like to put the problem on the family- or class-meeting agenda for problem-solving help during the next meeting. It can be most effective to ask children which of these suggestions they would find most helpful. Another possibility is to use your sense of humor: jump on top of both children while calling out "Pig pile", or place a make-believe microphone (your thumb) in front of one and then the other while claiming to be a TV newscaster—and then invite the "audience" to tune in tomorrow to see how these two young people use their problem-solving skills to find a solution.

Take Time to Train

ONE GOOD WAY to take time to train children is to get them involved in role-plays or "let's pretend." Teachers find it helpful to allow time for children to role-play solving hypothetical situations, such as conflict over use of playground equipment, shoving in line, name-calling, or fighting over a toy. Parents might help their children role-play appropriate ways to behave in a restaurant or a grocery store. Part of this training is to let children know what you will do if they don't behave. (See the next two tools.)

Decide What You Will Do

(SEE CHAPTER 7 for more information.) Of course, when you decide what you will do, children have to make decisions about what they will do. If you decide you won't drive while they are fighting (and then use the next three tools), children usually decide to stop fighting. Remember that it is important to let kids know in advance what you have decided.

Follow Through

(SEE CHAPTER 7 for more information.) Many parents complain that they don't want to have to follow through, yet they spend more time and wasted energy using punishment. Reread Chapter 7, accept that children don't always do what they promise to do, and then follow through. It is much more fun and much more effective.

Less Is More

(SEE CHAPTER 7 for more information.) Using the "less is more" philosophy is one way to follow through with kindness (by avoiding lectures and by keeping you mouth shut) and firmness (insisting on appropriate behavior). Some parents and teachers just don't believe they have done their job unless they punish or at least lecture. As I said earlier, adults are usually the only ones listening to their own lectures. Lectures usually create defensiveness in children, who will then stop listening.

Avoid "piggy backing," which means adding more (usually in the form of punishment or lectures) than what is effective to help a child learn from mistakes. Children listen more when you talk less or not at all. (See the next three tools.)

Use Nonverbal Signals

USING NONVERBAL SIGNALS is a great way to avoid words. It can also be fun for children—especially if they have helped create the nonverbal signal. You can create nonverbal signals for all kinds of things: a pillow case over the TV as a re-minder that chores need to be done; a hand over your heart that says, "I love you"; an empty plate turned over at the din-ner table as a reminder to wash hands first. Involving children in the creation of these signals is respectful and it increases their enthusiasm.

Say, "As soon as _____, then _____"

SAYING "AS SOON as your toys are picked, then we'll go to the park" is much more effective than, "If you pick up your toys, we'll go to the park." The first seems to invite cooperation. The second seems to invite a power struggle. Perhaps it is because the first phrase lets children know what you will do. The second option seems more like a manipulative bribe. Tone of voice and intent are important for this tool to be effective. It is best used when you don't have an investment in the outcome; for example, it is fine with you if you don't go to the park.

Teach Natural Consequences

A NATURAL CONSEQUENCE is something that happens because of a child's choice. It does not require adult interference. It is best if you do nothing except show empathy and support as children experience the consequences of their choices. After a cooling-off period, you might ask what and how questions to help children explore the consequences of their choices.

Teach Logical Consequences

REMEMBER, THIS IS a tool that is easily misunderstood. Avoid trying to disguise punishment by calling it a logical consequence. It may help to follow the Three Rs of Logical Consequences: Related, Respectful, and Reasonable to all concerned. The Three Rs can also apply to solutions.

Another question to ask yourself is, "Am I trying to make this child 'pay' for what he did, or am I trying to help him learn and change for the future?" Using the formula Opportunity = Responsibility = Consequence can help define when logical consequences might be appropriate. For every opportunity children have, there is a related responsibility. The obvious consequence for not accepting the responsibility is to lose the opportunity. A teenager who has the opportunity to use the family car may accept the responsibility for leaving the tank at least half full. When the tank is not half full, the consequence is to lose the use of the car for a previously agreed-upon time. This formula is effective only if the consequence is enforced respectfully, and children can regain the opportunity as soon as they show they are ready for the responsibility.

Use Encouragement Instead of Praise or Rewards

SEE THE CHART titled "Differences Between Praise and Encouragement" (page 152) for inspiration. Remember that encouragement motivates children from an inner locus of control while praise and rewards motivate them from an external locus of control.

Allowances Are Not Related to Chores

ALLOWANCES CAN BE a valuable tool to teach many important money management and other life skills. However, if allowances are related to chores, it becomes a matter of punishment (no allowance if chores are not done) and reward (if chores are done).

When you go to the store and your child cries for a toy, get to her eye level and ask if she has enough money saved from her allowance. If she says no, suggest, "You might want to save your money for that." You can even offer to save half. Children often lose interest if they have to save their money—even though they are always willing to spend yours.

Get Children Involved in Chores

JUST AS ALL children should have an allowance (no matter how small) just because they are part of the family, they should also do chores just because they are part of the family.

During family meetings, let children come up with plans for doing chores. You should have children revise their plans

Differences Between Praise and Encouragement

	PRAISE	ENCOURAGEMENT
Dictionary definition	1. To express a favorable *judgment* of 2. To glorify, especially by attribution of *perfection* 3. An expression of *approval*	1. To inspire with courage 2. To spur on; *stimulate*
Addresses	The doer: "Good girl."	The deed: "Good job."
Recognizes	Only complete, perfect product: "You did it right."	Effort and improvement: "You gave it your best" or "How do you feel about what you learned?"
Attitude	Patronizing, manipulative: "I like the way Suzie is sitting."	Respectful, appreciative: "Who can show me how we should be sitting now?"
"I" message	Judgmental: "I like the way you are sitting."	Self-disclosing: "I appreciate your cooperation."
Used most often with	Children: "You're such a good little girl."	Adults: "Thanks for helping."
Examples	"I'm proud of you for getting an A in math." (Robs person of ownership of own achievement.)	"That A reflects your hard work." (Recognizes ownership and responsibility for achievement.
Invites	People to change for others	People to change for themselves
Locus of control	External: "What do others think?"	Internal: "What do I think?"
Teaches	What to think; evaluation by others	How to think; self-evaluation
Goal	Conformity: "You did it right."	Understanding: "What do you think/feel/learn?"
Effect on self-esteem	Feel worthwhile only when others approve	Feel worthwhile without the approval of others
Long-range effect	Dependence on others	Self-confidence, self-reliance

Adapted from a chart by Judy Dixon and Bonnie Smith.

again and again. Children will often come up with a plan that will keep their enthusiasm for only a week or so. That simply means the issue needs to be discussed again. Sometimes children will come up with a new plan. Other times they will rededicate themselves to an old plan. Some plans have included placing in a jar strips of paper listing each chore. Children then draw out a few strips at each family meeting. Some children like chore charts with two rows of pockets (one row for chores that are not done, and one row for showing that a chore is completed). Some families have created a large circle of tag board with pictures of chores all around the edge of the circle. They attach a spinner to the center of the circle. Children then spin several times to find out what chores they will be doing for the week.

Give Hugs

THIS CAN BE the most simple, most fun, and sometimes the most effective tool of all. Of course, it doesn't work all the time. However, a simple hug can help a discouraged child feel encouraged. A hug can also help a frazzled parent change his or her attitude. A hug is often enough to help a child change from negative to positive behavior.

Provide Special Time

DOESN'T IT MAKE sense that spending special time with children is one of the best ways to help them develop perceptions of belonging and significance? If special time isn't scheduled, it usually doesn't happen. It can be very helpful to a child when you say, "I don't have time right now, but I'm looking forward to our special time at 6:45." Teachers have found that spending five minutes with a child during lunch or after school to discuss his or her favorite things to do can change a child's behavior dramatically.

One way to spend special time at the end of a bedtime routine is to ask your children (while tucking them in), "What is the saddest thing that happened to you today?" Listen and then share your sad time. Then ask, "What was the happiest thing that happened today?" Listen and share yours. This process gives parents the chance to hear things they might not hear if they didn't take this time, and it helps children feel belonging and significance. It also encourages children to look for happy times to share and to know that they will have undivided attention to share both happy and sad times of their day.

Use Positive Time-Out

EVEN THOUGH POSITIVE time-out is the main focus of this book, it cannot be omitted from a list of effective discipline tools.

You may be shaking your head by now and sighing, "This all sounds like an awful lot of work." There is no question that it is much easier for adults simply to tell children how to solve problems, rather than taking the time to allow them to develop and hone their own problem-solving skills. After all, children will make mistakes and errors of judgment, and we adults

When adults take the easy way out—going for short-range solutions rather than long-range teaching—they rob children of the opportunity to learn the skills the children so desperately need to survive and prosper in life.

know so much better. Still, when adults take the easy way out—going for short-range solutions rather than long-range teaching—they rob children of the opportunity to learn the skills they so desperately need to survive and prosper in life.

Take a closer look. Are these discipline methods really more work? Or, is it just that they challenge so many of our old beliefs about getting children to do what they should do through punishment and other controlling methods?

Thousands of parents and teachers have tried these methods and are thrilled with the results. They claim, "My children/students are not perfect, but they are so much better—and I now enjoy my job as a parent/teacher so much more."

11

Putting It All Together

I t has been said many times that punitive time-out may work for the moment, but lasting change requires much more. Children improve their behavior only when they feel encouraged, when they feel belonging and significance, and when they experience the kind of discipline that teaches them valuable life skills. Adults need to remember that discipline that teaches is an ongoing process.

The Long-Range Process

TYLER, A STUDENT in Mr. Lewis's fifth-grade class, habitually displayed extremely difficult behavior. He would lose his temper and become violent, hit other kids, knock over desks, and tear books. Mr. Lewis was at his wit's end. He felt he had tried everything: he had sent Tyler to the principal's office; he had made Tyler write one hundred sentences stating, "I will

not lose my temper in class"; and he had made Tyler stand outside the classroom door for punitive time-out.

Because Mr. Lewis's intention was to punish, none of these
tactics was effective. Tyler would be fine in the principal's office, but would come back to the classroom and soon lose his
temper again. After writing sentences about not losing his temper, he seemed more angry and volatile than ever. When he
was standing outside the classroom door, he would distract the
other students by making funny faces through the window.

Mr. Lewis decided to try a combination of the suggestions
outlined in this book. He started by changing his attitude to
one of dignity and respect instead of punishment and shame.

Mr. Lewis began the process by asking Tyler to stay after
school one day. With a friendly tone of voice, Mr. Lewis asked
Tyler if he had ever noticed what happened in his body when
he lost his temper? Tyler belligerently said, "No." (We need to
remember that it will take children a while to realize and trust
that we have changed our attitude. Tyler was used to being
punished and shamed and had his defenses up.)

Mr. Lewis continued in a calm and friendly manner by
sharing about himself. "Tyler, I lose my temper sometimes,
and I have noticed that when I'm paying attention to my body

at those times I can feel tension and stiffness in my neck." He grinned, "In other words, I get a pain in my neck." Mr. Lewis noticed Tyler was paying attention. (Mr. Lewis was admitting that he has the same problem Tyler has—that he sometimes loses his temper, which would, of course, interest Tyler.)

Mr. Lewis went on to ask Tyler if he would be willing to do a little experiment and pay attention to his body the next time he lost his temper to see what was happening. Tyler's manner still seemed a bit belligerent and suspicious, but he agreed.

Mr. Lewis shared that Tyler did not lose his temper for five days in a row—a record for him. It is my guess that the special time Mr. Lewis spent with Tyler helped him feel encouraged enough that he could suspend his misbehavior for a while. One-on-one sharing in a friendly manner can be very encouraging and empowering to a child.

On the sixth day, Tyler started fighting with another student. Mr. Lewis put his hand on Tyler's shoulder and whispered in his ear, "Did you notice what happened to your body? Come see me after school and tell me about it." That was enough to defuse the temper outburst, and Tyler went back to his desk with a thoughtful expression on his face.

> One-on-one sharing in a friendly manner can be very encouraging and empowering to a child.

After school, Tyler explained to Mr. Lewis that he noticed his hands clenched into a fist when he lost his temper and he felt like hitting something. (And, he usually acted on this feeling.) Mr. Lewis asked Tyler, "Would you be willing to use this information to create a plan that can help you control your temper so you will feel better about yourself? We can work on a plan together if you'd like." Tyler agreed.

The plan they agreed on was that whenever Tyler felt his hands clenching into a fist, he would step outside the classroom door and count to ten (or ten thousand), or look at the clouds and nature, or whatever it took to help him cool down and feel better. When he was ready, he could come back into the classroom. They agreed that he would not need to tell Mr. Lewis when he wanted to stand outside the door because he was working on self-control.

Again, Tyler did not have a temper tantrum for several days. On about the fifth day, Mr. Lewis noticed Tyler leave the classroom to stand outside the door. He stood there looking up at the sky. Mr. Lewis said, "I don't know if he was counting or just looking at the clouds, but it was different from when he would spend his time making faces through the window."

In about four minutes, Tyler came back into the classroom looking very satisfied with himself. Mr. Lewis went over to him, put his hand on his shoulder and said, "You handled that beautifully, Tyler. Way to go."

Mr. Lewis ended this story by saying, "I'm not going to tell you that Tyler never had another temper tantrum in class, because he did; however, he improved significantly. He used to have three or four tantrums a week. Now he has two or three a month. I'll take it!"

Improvement Is a Lifelong Process

WE NEED TO remember that perfectionism is extremely discouraging. Adults often seem to expect more from children than adults can accomplish themselves. How many of us are still working on something, such as being on time, losing weight, controlling our temper, or other areas where we might improve, but never obtain perfection? It took time for Mr.

We need to remember that perfectionism is extremely discouraging. Adults often seem to expect more from children than adults can accomplish themselves.

Lewis to work with Tyler (but no more time than he had spent on punishment), but the results were worth it. It also taught Tyler some important skills that he could use throughout his life.

Work on Improvement, Not Perfection

MR. LEWIS CONTINUED to work with Tyler regularly. When Tyler would lose his temper, Mr. Lewis would see him after school and remind him how much he had improved. Mr. Lewis even told Tyler that he had been an inspiration to him, "I have controlled my temper better by watching how well you do, but I'm not perfect yet either."

There are many methods—both short-range and long-range—that work to change misbehavior and improve children's self-esteem. Positive time-out can help improve behavior without sacrificing self-esteem.

The Power of Love

YOU HAVE PROBABLY heard it before, but it always bears repeating: Never underestimate the power of love. What matters most in life to children is knowing that the important people in their lives—parents, teachers, family, friends—love them and believe in their intrinsic worth as human beings.

> P ositive time-
> out can help
> improve behavior
> without sacrificing
> self-esteem.

Of course, children aren't consciously aware of this deep need, nor can they always verbalize it; yet they always know somehow when the need to belong and to be loved hasn't been met. This need carries over to school, too. Research shows that the main predictor of a child's achievement in school is his or her perception of "Does the teacher *like* me?"

Betsy Licciardello, a teacher of special education in Roseville, California, beautifully illustrates the power of love in the following story:

> *I've taught special education for ten years. I heard Jane Nelsen speak four or five years ago and began incorporating her positive-discipline approach at home and at school.*
>
> *This year I have a little girl in class who comes from an abusive home. She suffers from severe self-esteem problems. She also wet and soiled her pants daily at school. My aide and I tried many solutions. We cleaned her up—she adored the attention. We had her clean herself up—no improvement. We tried hugs for dry pants every half-hour and had very inconsistent results.*
>
> *One day, as I was walking this girl to the office for dry socks (she had soaked herself all the way to her shoes), I decided just to tell her how I felt about her. I told her, "I love you and will always love you, no matter what you do— good days or bad. I will love you even if you wet your pants every day or if you never wet your pants again. I like dry pants better, but I will love you no matter what you choose—wet pants or dry."*

She hasn't wet her pants at school since we had this little talk. We have the talk every once in awhile as a reminder, and we still have lots of hugs. We no longer have wet pants. Hooray!

The most important part of this story is that Betsy really meant it when she said she would love this little girl even if she continued to wet her pants. Betsy didn't just pretend or use a declaration of love to manipulate change. It's important to realize that children can almost always tell the difference. Change is often inspired by unconditional love, freely offered. Betsy understands the power of love. May her story be an inspiration to others.

The Real World

ADULTS WOULD UNDOUBTEDLY be much happier if the children in their care never misbehaved or felt the need for time-out. But this is the real world, and we're all human—adults and children alike. Mood swings, bad days, stress, and unforeseen catastrophes are a fact of life for all of us. Consistent use of encouragement and positive, empowering ways of interacting with one another can help children feel sufficient belonging and significance so that they rarely need time-out. Teaching children (and adults!) the value of positive time-out as an opportunity to catch their breath, calm down, and feel better, or to evaluate and learn from their experiences through the what and how questions, is a gift that can serve them throughout their lives.

If we're honest, most of us will admit that we long to feel in control of our lives, and especially of our children. Although locking children in boxes, withdrawing privileges that have nothing to do with the misbehavior, spanking, shaking, and other forms of punishment may give us the illusion of being in control for the moment, the long-range results are never in the best interests of children or of society as a whole.

Social Interest

ALFRED ADLER BELIEVED that mental health, including self-esteem, is directly related to the amount of social interest one has. *Social interest* means the genuine interest we have in others and in our social community. When we're not feeling healthy or good about who we are, we tend to withdraw from relationships and from our community. This is a lack of social interest, and children, as well as adults, experience it.

Problem-solving skills help children to be interested in others and to respect differences. Group problem solving (such as family or class meetings) teaches the importance of social interest and problem-solving skills in the community of family or classroom.

What Do You Really Want for Your Children?

ASK A GROUP of parents what they really want for their children, and they'll usually tell you they want their children to be happy. Ask them what sort of adults they want those children to become, and they have to think a bit harder, but they'll eventually come up with qualities like responsible, independent, wise, confident, compassionate, kind, honest, respectful, and industrious.

Those qualities don't just happen; we have to build them into our children from their earliest days, and yes, it takes a lot of hard work. It is worth remembering, too, that parents are only human; we all make mistakes more often than we would

Alfred Adler believed that mental health, including self-esteem, is directly related to the amount of social interest one has. *Social interest* means the genuine interest we have in others and in our social community.

like. But a relationship that is built on love, trust, encouragement, and hope will endure an amazing number of mistakes. A relationship with our children that is based on mutual dignity and respect carries a price; but aren't our children worth the effort?

Building the Relationship

AMONG THE GREATEST keys to building trust, confidence, and problem-solving abilities are communication, the art of listening, respect, and love. Because the primary goal of children is to achieve a sense of belonging and significance, what better way to help them feel those things than by spending time listening, understanding, and helping them feel appreciated and loved?

We live in a busy world, and the number of tasks that need to be done can easily overwhelm parents and teachers. Sometimes the rush and stress of daily life stretches our relationships with those we love to the breaking point. No single technique of discipline or behavior management will solve our problems.

Sometimes children resort to attention-getting misbehaviors because they have a legitimate *need* for focused attention from the adults in their lives. Shaping behavior and encouraging life skills goes beyond time-out, logical consequences, or family meetings; it requires time, patience, love, and understanding.

It helps to remember that children's needs are much like ours. We want to feel that our contributions are noticed, that someone cares about what we've done or how we feel, that someone loves us (and so do our children). Taking time just to *listen* with undivided attention, to get down on a child's level and make eye contact when we speak, to use friendly touches and hugs as well as words to communicate love and affection are all very powerful tools. The following is an example of this situation.

Janice was in the midst of an important business call when her six-year-old daughter Meg came home from school. It had been a hectic day—Janice was behind in her work, the house was a mess, and laundry was spilling out of the hamper. Janice still had to arrange for child care in order to attend a meeting that evening, and her nerves were close to fraying.

Meg, on the other hand, had had a wonderful day at school and wanted to share it with her mother, who had seemed more distracted and tense than usual lately. There hadn't been much time for reading, story telling, or simply being together. Today Meg had a really neat picture that she had painted all by herself; she couldn't wait to show her mom.

"Mom," she said excitedly, tugging at Janice's sleeve, "Mom, look at my picture."

"Excuse me," Janice said into the receiver; then, to Meg, "Not now, Meg; can't you see I'm on the phone? You know our rules about that."

But Meg couldn't wait. "Mom," she persisted, more loudly this time. "Mom, I want to show you my picture!"

Her mom, completely exasperated now, said, more angrily than she'd intended, "Obviously, Meg, you can't seem to follow our rules. You'd better go to your room for some time-out until you feel better!"

Meg, lower lip trembling, disappeared. And Janice, whose phone call finally ended, collapsed on the couch with a sigh. After a moment of time-out for herself, she walked into her daughter's room to find Meg sitting dejectedly on the floor, looking at a book.

> Taking time just to *listen* with undivided attention, to get down on a child's level and make eye contact when we speak, to use friendly touches and hugs as well as words to communicate love and affection are all very powerful tools.

Janice gently turned the little girl until she could look directly into her eyes and lovingly stroked her cheek. "You're feeling pretty disappointed, aren't you?" she asked Meg. Meg, lower lip now trembling violently, nodded. "I know I've been too busy lately, and we haven't had much time together. And I've been feeling really stressed, and I know that makes me impatient. Would you forgive me for losing my temper? And would you show me your picture? I really do want to see it, you know."

Meg and Janice sat down together on the bed to examine the picture Meg had painted. Afterward, they talked for a while and then ate a cozy dinner together. Although Janice still had to leave for her meeting, she arranged with her daughter for a special time together that weekend, and they shared a big hug.

Meg was sent to time-out when Janice needed it more than Meg did. When Janice had time to calm down, she realized this. Once she reestablished the love and trust, she worked with Meg on creating a positive time-out area. They decided on a special signal (just like the one sports referees use) that would remind each other that some time-out was needed. After the signal was given, they would decide who would be helped the most by time-out and if they would like to go alone or together.

Sometimes our expectations for ourselves, our family life, and those we love are unrealistically high; we need to realize that children, like adults, will have grumpy days and bad moods, and misbehavior will never completely disappear. Still, by working on encouragement and positive ways of relating to our children, including the positive use of time-out, we can not only help them control their behavior, but also give them the self-control and self-esteem to tackle life with confidence.

BIBLIOGRAPHY

Dreikurs, Rudolf, with Vicki Soltz. *Children: The Challenge.* New York: Plume Books, 1990.

Kamii, Constance. Obedience is not enough. *Young Children* May 1984, 11–14.

Kohn, Alfred. *Punished by Rewards.* New York: Houghton-Mifflin, 1993.

Nelsen, Jane. *Positive Discipline.* New York: Ballantine, 1996.

Nelsen, Jane; Roslyn Duffy; Linda Escobar; Kate Ortolano; and Debbie Owen-Sohocki. *Positive Discipline: A Teacher's A–Z Guide.* Rocklin, CA: Prima Publishing, 1996.

Nelsen, Jane; Cheryl Erwin; and Carol Delzer. *Positive Discipline for Single Parents,* 2nd ed. Rocklin, CA: Prima Publishing, 1999.

Nelsen, Jane; Cheryl Erwin; and Roslyn Duffy. *Positive Discipline for Preschoolers.* Rocklin, CA: Prima Publishing, 1998.

Nelsen, Jane; Cheryl Erwin; and Roslyn Duffy. *Positive Discipline: The First Three Years.* Rocklin, CA: Prima Publishing, 1998.

Nelsen, Jane; Cheryl Erwin; and H. Stephen Glenn. *Positive Discipline for Blended Families.* Rocklin, CA: Prima Publishing, 1997.

Nelsen, Jane; Lynn Lott; and Riki Intner. *Positive Discipline for Parenting in Recovery.* Rocklin, CA: Prima Publishing, 1996.

Nelsen, Jane; and Lynn Lott. *Positive Discipline for Teenagers,* 2nd ed. Rocklin, CA: Prima Publishing, 2000.

Nelsen, Jane; Lynn Lott; and H. Stephen Glenn. *Positive Discipline A–Z,* 2nd ed. Rocklin, CA: Prima Publishing, 1999.

Nelsen, Jane; Lynn Lott; and H. Stephen Glenn. *Positive Discipline in the Classroom,* 2nd ed. Rocklin, CA: Prima Publishing, 2000.

Piaget, Jane. *The Moral Judgment of Children.* Trans. Marjorie Gabain. New York: Free Press, 1965.

Taylor, John. *Person to Person: Awareness Techniques for Counselors, Group Leaders, and Parent Educators.* Saratoga, CA: R&E Publishers, 1984.

Tronick, E. Z., and A. Gianino. Zero to three. *Bulletin for the National Center for Critical Infant Programs* 6(3): 1–6.

INDEX

FOR MORE INFORMATION

Workshops, seminars, and parent facilitator training are scheduled throughout the United States each year. For dates and location or to schedule a workshop for your organization, contact:

Empowering People
P.O. Box 1926
Orem, UT 84059-1926
1-800-456-7770
Email: JaneNelsen@aol.com
Web site: www.positivediscipline.com

The author also provides dynamic lectures, corporate seminars, and conference keynote presentations. For more information, or to schedule a presentation or workshop, call 1-800-456-7770.

ORDER FORM

To: Empowering People, P.O. Box 1926, Orem, UT 84059-1926
Phone: 1-800-456-7770 (credit card orders only)
Fax: 801-762-0022
Web Site: www.positivediscipline.com for discount prices

BOOKS	Price	Quantity	Amount
Positive Discipline for Your Stepfamily, by Nelsen, Erwin, & Glenn	$16.95		
Positive Discipline for Single Parents, by Nelsen, Erwin, & Delzer	$16.95		
Positive Discipline in the Classroom, by Nelsen, Lott, & Glenn	$16.95		
Positive Discipline: A Teacher's A–Z Guide, by Nelsen, Duffy, Escobar, Ortolano, & Owen-Sohocki	$16.95		
Positive Discipline for Preschoolers, by Nelsen, Erwin, & Duffy	$16.95		
Positive Discipline: The First Three Years, by Nelsen, Erwin, & Duffy	$16.95		
Positive Discipline, by Nelsen	$12.00		
Positive Discipline A–Z, by Nelsen, Lott, & Glenn	$16.95		
Positive Discipline for Teenagers, by Nelsen & Lott	$16.95		
Positive Discipline for Parenting in Recovery, by Nelsen, Intner, & Lott	$12.95		
Raising Self-Reliant Children in a Self-Indulgent World, by Glenn & Nelsen	$15.95		
Positive Time-Out: And 50 Other Ways to Avoid Power Struggles, Nelsen	$12.95		
From Here to Serenity, by Nelsen	$14.00		
Positive Discipline in the Christian Home, by Nelsen, Erwin, Brock & Hughes	$16.95		
Positive Discipline for Childcare Providers, by Nelsen & Erwin	$16.95		

MANUALS	Price	Quantity	Amount
Teaching Parenting the Positive Discipline Way, by Lott & Nelsen	$49.95		
Positive Discipline in the Classroom, by Nelsen & Lott	$49.95		

TAPES AND VIDEOS	Price	Quantity	Amount
Positive Discipline audiotape	$10.00		
Positive Discipline videotape	$49.95		
Building Healthy Self-Esteem Through Positive Discipline audiotape	$10.00		

SUBTOTAL _____

Sales tax: UT add 6.25%; CA add 7.25% _____

Shipping & handling: $3.00 plus $0.50 each item _____

(Prices subject to change without notice.) **TOTAL** _____

METHOD OF PAYMENT (check one):
_____ Check made payable to Empowering People Books, Tapes, & Videos
_____ MasterCard, Visa, Discover Card, American Express

Card # _____ Expiration _____ / _____
Ship to _____
Address _____
City/State/Zip _____
Daytime phone (_____)_____

ABOUT THE AUTHOR

 JANE NELSEN is a popular lecturer and co-author of the entire POSITIVE DISCIPLINE series. She has appeared on *Oprah* and *Sally Jesse Raphael* and was the featured parent expert on the *National Parent Quiz,* hosted by Ben Vereen. Jane is the mother of seven children and the grandmother of seventeen.